REVIEWS & PRAISE

Sharing one's life story is not easy to do. But in this case the reason to share the story is to encourage other people who have gone through similar pain. I appreciate Sarah's sharing her journey. I have watched this story of healing emerge over the years as God has done healing work in lives and families. I commend her story to those who are dealing with their own pain and those who like to read biography.
David Harvey ~ Acts 12:24 Churches Superintendent

In meeting Sarah a few years ago it only took a short time to realize her life is lived for Jesus. It was an honor to review her book, reading almost her entire story in one sitting because I couldn't put it down. I cried, completely undone by how Sarah has chosen to use her brokenness for His glory. Jesus really does make everything beautiful. Through the pages of her very hard story, Sarah challenges you to see your brokenness through a lens of hope and grace.
Susan Kemmerer ~ Author and motivational speaker

The incredible, sustaining, transformational power of the love of God is irrefutable in the still developing story of the life of this author. Only the hand of God could have kept her and taught her through the worst pain and confusion imaginable and used this young woman to become a vessel of that love to bring healing and freedom to so many other lives. Be prepared to experience suspense, shattering heartbreak, and awe-inspiring victory as you enter Sarah's world. Even after knowing her for 25 years, I am more in awe of the gifted, capable, hardworking, creative, joyful woman Sarah has become through forgiveness.

Debbie Rogers ~ Para-Educator, Prayer Warrior

Sarah's journey back to restoration included many tears as she faced the trauma of her past, but she was met on that journey by the God described in Psalm 56:8 "You (God) keep track of all my sorrows. You have collected all my tears in your bottle. You have recorded each one in your book." The same God has been collecting your tears and is ready to help you on your own journey back to restoration. Allow Sarah's story to inspire courage in you to seek God for healing in your life. You can join the multitudes of people who have experienced that joy and peace in God that leads us all to the ultimate reality of Revelation 21:4 "He (God) will wipe every tear from their eyes, and there will be no more death or sorrow or crying or pain. All these things are gone forever."

Pastor Mike Matthews

I met Sarah as she was helping families clean up after a hurricane. She was being the hands and feet of Jesus as she served with Samaritans Purse. Having now read her story I ask how. How after all that she has been through in her life is she the loving, giving, smiling person I met serving the Lord by caring for others? How is that possible? I can only answer, God! Only God can change a life and give back what sin has taken away!

Dan Halstead ~ Friend and volunteer team lead with Samaritans Purse

"Restoration"—for some is renewal, some renovation, for others it is a complete rebuilding of their lives. It's ironic that Sarah's book, <u>A Journey Back to Restoration</u>, was set to be released while she was here in Houston helping to rebuild lives shattered by the impact of an unwelcomed visitor, Hurricane Harvey. Children today in foster care have had their lives shattered through abuse, abandonment, and neglect which often leads to sex-trafficking or exploitation. Sarah's story is one of overcoming. She demonstrates impressive strength to take this journey of restoration. While she tells about it in her book, she serves as one who gives hope, brings joy in the midst of despair, and fights the hard fight. Foster children, like the children we serve at Arrow Child & Family Ministries, need her story. We all need her story to know what these kids face and how to help them overcome. Sarah's book allows us to step into their lives and take the journey back to restoration. Her story compels us to keep reading and see the hope, the joy, and the forgiveness that is possible...even from the darkest places. We are grateful for her overcoming attitude and her strength to take the journey. Be encouraged as you read, knowing you will not be disappointed.

Scott Lundy ~ CEO, Arrow Child & Family Ministries

A Journey Back to Restoration

A Story of Healing & Forgiveness
A Story of Blessings, Peace, & Joy

Sarah Isaac-Samuel

Powerful You!
PUBLISHING
Sharing Wisdom ~ Shining Light

A JOURNEY BACK TO RESTORATION
A Story of Healing & Forgiveness
A Story of Blessings, Peace, & Joy

Copyright © 2018

Published by: Powerful You! Inc. USA
powerfulyoupublishing.com

Library of Congress Control Number: 2018952830

Sarah Isaac-Samuel – First Edition

ISBN: 978-0-9970661-9-7

First Edition September 2018

MEMOIR / SELF-HELP / INSPIRATION

DEDICATION

This book is dedicated to my family
for supporting me through the many difficult times.

To my dear friend Dawn,
who encouraged me to never give up and who will always
bring me a bag of yarn.

To Josephine and Heidi,
that they may find healing in the truth.

And, last but certainly not least, Emily,
for walking with me and sharing in the healing process.

TABLE OF CONTENTS

FOREWORD
By Linda Adams

Family. Home. Belonging. I grew up inhabiting these comforting words every day of my life, taking for granted the good feelings they brought.

Knowing Sarah as a lovely and lively woman, I would never have guessed that her birth family and many subsequent "families" had abused, abandoned, and betrayed her as a young and vulnerable child. Yet she opened her heart in a classroom setting, telling her own story in a riveting way, captivating her listeners. In just a few minutes, she introduced us to the world she had known as a girl and how one surreal event led to another and another in a downward spiral. We experienced her feelings of helplessness, confusion, and pain. It dawned on us that her reality is horribly familiar to countless other adults, teens, and children in America and around the world.

Now Sarah has embarked on the courageous journey of healing and has written her life story in intimate detail as a step in that process. Her growth as a woman of faith and integrity has led her to help others find their way along a similar path by offering a window into her own soul. She knows restoration is possible, because she lives the healing journey every day.

Live Sarah's story through this book. Feel the sting of injustice in a violent parent's torture. Wonder how adults can inflict such cruelty. Consider the complex role of all the social workers, foster parents, educators, pastors, and counselors whose job it was to help her. Let your heart experience life through the eyes of a little girl who became a troubled teen, and then find a way to get on the solution side of this enormous challenge in our day, as she has done.

AUTHOR'S NOTE

All the events in this story are real and can be found in public court documents, medical records, and other government agencies. However, I chose to write this book in a way that protects the identity and privacy of those involved. The intention of this book is not to show blame, but to tell my story in order that others may be encouraged to find healing.

INTRODUCTION

On my wall hangs a plaque that reads "What lies behind us and what lies before us are small matters compared to what lies within us." ~ Ralph Waldo Emerson

For individuals trying to find healing from past abuse this concept can seem foreign because what lies behind or before them is no small matter. What they may not realize is the importance of what lies within them because that is the key for millions of people in the world suffering the pain of abuse, neglect, or abandonment. One of the worst "side effects" of this pain is the feeling of isolation; most people don't realize how many others are dealing with the same issues because they are too ashamed to talk about what happened to them.

So many people keep their true selves hidden for fear that others will judge them. The thoughts tend to go something like this: *If others find out [insert secret] about me, they might not think I'm a nice person.* Or, *they may look down on me and will no longer be my friend.* While it may seem easier to live this way than go through more hurt and rejection, the truth is when we don't share our pain with others we are giving it free rein to fester and cause even greater damage to who God created us to be. It certainly makes it harder to let the pain go, and while we're trying desperately to manage our pain and present a brave face to the world, the person who hurt us is moving on. They may not even be thinking about what happened or what they did to us.

What I've come to realize is that each person deals with trauma differently. Some need to know everything that happened in order to process it. Others suppress it and bury it so they don't have to think about it. Still others have a mechanism that completely blocks it from their mind as if it never happened because the pain is too unbearable to deal with.

Everyone heals differently as well. It can take two years or twenty; in some cases it is an instantaneous transformation – what we usually refer to as a "miracle." It all depends on the individual and the circumstances that got them to the place they are now. The truth is that all healings are miraculous, no matter how long they take, and if we allow God into our hearts and lives, there is nothing He will not be with us through. I know, because this happened for me.

The LORD is near to the brokenhearted and saves those who are crushed in spirit. ~ Psalm 34:18 NAS

***

What follows is the story of a girl who grew up having to move from place to place, and the abuse she sustained throughout her adolescent years. It's a story of pain and suffering, but it's also a story of forgiveness, healing, love, and acceptance. Most of all, it's a story of what God can do in a person's life if only He's given the opportunity.

This is my story, given to me by God.

Can a mother forget the baby at her breast and have no compassion on the child she has borne? Though she may forget, I will not forget you! See, I have engraved you on the palms of my hands; your walls are ever before me. ~ *Isaiah 49:15-16 NIV*

The Beginning

As I sit down to write this story, it is difficult not to get overwhelmed. My mind sifts through countless memories, trying to find a starting point, and just when I'm convinced I'm not going to find one, I circle back to that warm summer day, and traveling that winding dirt road so deep in the middle of nowhere that if you didn't know where it was you'd pass right by it. The trees are beautiful and full, and the sun warms the air. The road eventually opens into a large meadow, in the center of which is a rundown farmhouse. As I see the house, I realize it's familiar to me, though I can't say I've ever been there. It's almost as if I've seen it in a dream. Then I hear my mom say, "This is the house we lived in when you were born." Immediately my heart sinks, and the beauty seems to fade away as the painful memories flood my mind.

I know I shouldn't be so surprised. My oldest sister Josephine and I had decided it was time to try and piece together our past and, hopefully, put it to rest. We'd enlisted our mother's help in finding some key places, the location of which we weren't sure of. This was all part of the plan. I just hadn't anticipated how strongly I would react.

Even though I was too young to remember this farmhouse, I instinctively knew something important had happened here. One wintry day early in my second year, our mother had decided living with us and our father was too much to handle. The events surrounding her departure were unclear, but I'd often wondered how a mother could leave three young children behind, an infant and two toddlers.

At that moment, as I sat next to her in the car, it was all I could do to keep my composure. All I'd ever wanted to know was why, and yet she still couldn't explain it. Maybe it was too hard for her to relive that time. Maybe she felt guilty. Whatever the case, I knew we might not ever learn the whole story about that day. All I knew was that it had left a very painful scar.

I would eventually forgive my mother, but as we stared at the farmhouse, that forgiveness was still far in the future. The anger and frustration roiled in my gut, and my mind flashed back, which took me back to another, more recent, memory, when the events of my childhood threatened to destroy the life I had built with my own husband and children.

It was autumn, and a dark time in my life. Depression had set in and brought with it a host of physical problems. I was in constant pain with limited range of motion in my legs. Knowing I needed help, I turned to the leader of a support group I'd been attending. She got me in contact with a hospital that was several states away.

Immediately, my thoughts went to my daughters—Naomi, who was four, and Elizabeth, almost two. How could I do this to them? I was almost two when my mother left and here I was, about to leave my daughter at the same tender age. As awful as I felt, I knew that if I didn't get help for myself it would be worse for them in the long run. Before I left, I made arrangements for child care and made sure my husband Charlie didn't have to worry about the bills or any household issues. My issues—whatever they were—had caused him enough stress.

Through it all I felt God telling me, "It's okay, all will be fine." I had to trust that feeling, or I would have continued in a downward-spiraling cycle.

I spent the next month in daily counseling, and my own

mother's abandonment quickly came to the forefront. During one session, the counselor said it was time to call Mom and confront the issue head on.

As I dialed the number, my anxiety grew. My mother and I were not in regular contact at that time, and in fact I still held a lot of unresolved anger toward her. She was not even aware that I was in the hospital, and I had no idea what to expect from the phone call. I didn't realize at the time that my healing depended not on her reaction, but in my ability to speak my truth and then let it go.

After explaining the reason for my call, I asked her, "How could you leave three young children like that, and was I potty trained?"

While this question may seem odd to some, it directly went to the questions I'd always had about the circumstances surrounding her departure, and exactly how helpless me and my sisters were. I had been told my father was not home at the time—were we able to tend to our own bathroom needs, or did we have to sit there for hours, waiting to be changed? The thought of this really bothered me, particularly since it is a basic need that most mothers are diligent about. Heidi, just eight months old, definitely was not trained. I was told my mother had left during a blizzard, which at least gave me a reference point from which to research. There was indeed a record blizzard that caused more than two hundred deaths. I'd also been told she left on her birthday, which according to what I'd read had occurred three days after the storm ended; however, there was still a huge amount of snow that she would have had to trudge through in order to be able to reach a paved road.   Apparently, she had been desperate to escape.

Now, after all these years, I couldn't believe I finally had the chance to ask her directly. Unfortunately though I had steeled myself for the response, it was still a shock.

"I never said I was the motherly type."

I held the phone, speechless, my mind struggling to reconcile her words with the all-encompassing feeling of love I had for my own children. I did not get my answers that day; in fact, I still do not know how long we were alone or whether Josephine and I were still in diapers.

Until this point, I had managed to persevere despite my physical discomfort. Shortly after that conversation with my mother I woke up one morning, my body still as a board and in terrible agony. The doctors and nurses were alerted, and when they came into my room they found me curled in the fetal position and sobbing uncontrollably. It was surreal—I couldn't speak or move, just listened to them talking about having to get me a special bed.

Silently, I started praying to God to help me get through this. After about thirty minutes, things started to change. A vision came upon me, and I saw God standing there by my bed in all His majesty. He reached down and gently picked me up, and I truly felt as though I was lying in the hands of Jesus. It was as if I were an infant cradled in my Father's arms. I felt nothing but pure love. This vision was suddenly replaced by another: an image of the entire world held in the hands of God. I came to a realization of how BIG He really is and how much He really loves us. Peace encompassed me, and I felt whole again, as if I could take on the world. The doctors and nurses watched in amazement as I got up out of the bed and walked around, completely pain-free.

A few days later I sat with my doctor, discussing my return home. He stepped from the room for a moment and left my chart open on the desk. Unable to resist a peek, I glanced at it to see what type of notes he had written about me. The words "unexplained healing" stood out to me in bold relief. I had a very good explanation, though: God had heard my prayers and took away my pain.

A week later I was released. I went home and was reunited with Charlie and the girls. Things were not perfect, but at least we knew now what was going on in my head and had an idea of how to deal with it.

Now, as I sat there in the car with my mother, I once again prayed for God's help.

"It's okay," He told me, "All will be fine."

Sure enough, I managed to keep my emotions and tongue in check, and we proceeded with our journey.

The next stop couldn't be as hard. After all we remembered the place and the fun we had playing with our cousins. But could we even find it? After driving over the mountain we headed down an open stretch of paved road and eventually came upon an ugly trailer sitting in a small plot of trees with nothing but open fields all around. It seemed so out of place and reminded me of something you would find in a junkyard. As we sat there looking at this ugly green mass it was hard to imagine that such a large family could have fit in such a small trailer. They had six children and two adults and when we stayed with our cousins there were another three children. My sister and I exchange glances.

Did we really play here?

We pulled off the side of the road, and Josephine and I reminisced about the fun we'd had as young children. We climbed trees and played hide and seek; sometimes we just played in the dirt and watched the migrant workers in the cotton fields. After our visit to the farmhouse, it was a relief to remember something good about a childhood that had always felt so sad and hurtful.

Finally, and with great reluctance, we pulled away. As much as I would have liked to stay by the not-so-beautiful structure all day, I knew there were many more places to see, many more memories to revisit.

That's What Happens

As my mom, Josephine and I traveled the back roads through the countryside, we talked of growing up and the difficult times. Less than a year after Mom left us that stormy winter day, our lives were upended once again when our father was sent to prison for armed robbery and larceny. We never learned the whole story there either, but my siblings and I went to live with our paternal grandparents.

Much of that time lived as blurry thoughts in our heads, but as we discussed it Josephine and I did recall an old picture of the two of us, dressed in matching jackets, walking up a hill. We looked like twins. I also remembered playing out front of the house and finding colorful tile pieces strewn here and there. Every time I found one I felt I had found a beautiful treasure.

We talked about how we had to take naps on the floor in the living room. My younger sister Heidi laid on one side, Josephine on the other, and I was always in the middle facing someone's back. We remembered the old picture of Jesus in the Garden that hung on the wall in a metal frame and the black panther figurine on the shelf.

Like most little kids, we took enjoyment in some of life's ordinary tasks. We loved climbing up on the step stool to help with the dishes. We also weren't fazed by life's inconveniences. Back then our grandparents' house did not have an indoor bathroom; we had to make trips to an outhouse, kept buckets by our bedsides for nighttime, and took our baths in an old metal tub that had to be filled by hand.

Josephine and I laughed as we reminisced about these things, which now seemed like scenes from a very old movie.

Our minds went to the days we spent helping in the garden patch at the end of the property, and how we could walk down a path and through the tall thin trees that hid our uncle's house, where we would occasionally go to play.

I then remembered the morning we woke up to people talking in hushed voices. Though I was only three, I knew something was off. Then someone came to us and explained that our grandfather had died in his sleep the night before. I don't remember really feeling anything, for I didn't understand the concept of death. I do recall wanting to see him but not being allowed in his room.

Mom, Josephine, and I were still talking about it when we came to the top of the hill overlooking our grandparents' home. It had new owners now, so we just parked the car at the top of the hill and peered down through the trees and overgrown weeds.

Things got quiet, and that churning feeling inside my gut started to come back. *Is this what it's going to be like all day*, I wondered, but I already knew the answer.

I remembered one day shortly after my grandfather died. I was sitting on the front porch playing with a doll. I stared down at her and thought, *How does this hair stay in the head of the doll?* I started pulling out her hair to figure it out.

When our grandmother came out and saw what I was doing, she got very upset. She took hold of my arm and brought me into the kitchen. In the middle of the kitchen was an old kerosene heater. She grabbed my hands and held them over the heater. The tears began to flow as the pain grew unbearable.

After what seemed like forever, she took my hands off and

said, "That's what happens to little girls who destroy their dolls."

By this time my hands were burnt and blistered. Grandmother put a healing balm on the palms of my hands and bandaged them so they would heal. Shortly after that, a woman we had never seen before showed up at the house. Her name was Molly, she said, and she was our father's new girlfriend. She was going to take care of us until my father got out of prison.

A few years ago I heard there was a fire at our grandparents' house and went to see it. It had completely burnt to the ground. The smoldering ash smell still lingered in the air, and it felt rather eerie to be standing there. Next to the pile of ashes sat an old doghouse. Beautiful bee balm was blooming around it. I thought to myself what beauty in the midst of such devastation. Maybe this is what God meant when He tells us to focus our minds on things that are pure and lovely.

I didn't speak much as we stared at my grandparents' home; I was too busy reliving the agony of my burnt hands and the anxiety of having to once again go off to another home. *Okay,* I told myself, *you really need to keep it together.* If I didn't, I wouldn't be able to continue, and then the whole trip would have been a waste. As we headed into town for our next stop, I prayed it would not be as difficult, and that whatever we encountered, I would have the strength to endure it.

The New Girlfriend

Though we kept the conversation light, my anxiety continued to grow as we drew closer to the place we'd lived with Molly. What had I been thinking? How could the memories get easier when the events had gotten progressively worse? We finally arrived at the small home and parked across the street so we could observe and talk, but instead a silence fell over the car. Memories flooded my mind and my stomach once again rose up in revolt.

It was Josephine who broke the silence; she recalled us carrying pots of water to the end of the yard where the dog was. The water would end up freezing, and he'd have nothing to drink. She reminded me how we walked to school and played in the alley on the way home, and of the corner store, where we stopped for penny candy. We talked about the babysitter around the corner, and how scary her neighbor was, then we fell silent again. There didn't seem to be any other good memories.

Once again I was sifting through the past, from the days we lived in this house. There was a flash of the attic, and the incident that had happened there. I asked my sister if she remembered the red polka dot dresses. She said she remembered the pictures of us wearing them, but they held no significance for her. This was when I realized that although Josephine was a year older (I was four when we lived with Molly and she was five), she didn't remember as much as I did about what had happened to us.

On the days Molly worked, she would arrange for a sitter

to come over. This particular day, our cousin Eugene had agreed to watch us until she returned. What he hadn't prepared for was Molly returning home early because she was sick.

I don't remember hearing her come into the house, just the sound of her voice when she got upstairs, then, Eugene, urging us to hurry up and get dressed. He had taken us up into the attic and was sexually molesting both of us. We struggled to get into our clothes, but not before Molly walked in.

The next few minutes flew by in an angry blur. Molly started screaming at Eugene to get out, and though I don't remember exactly what she said I know she threatened him. She told me and Josephine to go to our room, and we sat on the end of our beds, listening to the sound of Eugene running from the house with Molly on his heels. A few minutes later she came back inside, but she did not speak to us about what had happened, which only added to our fear and confusion.

Shortly after that we had these brand new red polka dot dresses with large white collars that reminded me of a bib. I wasn't really fond of the collar, but I really liked having a new dress.

Molly escorted us into this huge building with a large foyer and fancy staircases. We walked up to the second floor and into an office with a guard in it. A few minutes later, another person in uniform came and took my sister away. I was to wait with the guard until they were ready for me.

A little while later I was taken into an enormous room filled with benches and lots of people. I felt their eyes on me as I was brought in the side door near a man sitting in a black robe. In a gentle tone, he introduced himself as Judge So-and-So, then asked me my name before telling the guard to sit me up on the front of his desk. That's when I noticed Eugene, sitting a few feet away. "Are you afraid?" the judge asked, and I told him, "No." He told me they were going to ask me some questions, and all I had to do was answer them as best I could. He was a very nice man. He told me when it was over, they would take me back into the office room and give me a lollipop. I was excited about that.

I really don't remember the questions, except when they asked whether the person who'd hurt me was in the room and if so, if I could point to that person. After I'd pointed out Eugene, the judge thanked me and told me I'd done a great job. They took me to the office and gave me my lollipop as promised. I remember feeling like I had done something important that day, but I wasn't sure what.

My mind went back to that same fall when I was hospitalized. Though I didn't know much about triggers at the time, it was no coincidence that my daughter Elizabeth was almost two—the same age I was when my mother left, and Naomi was four—the age I was when Eugene molested me.

In fact, the reason I was even in a support group at the time was because I was haunted by the memories of what happened in the attic that day.

As we sat in the car across from Molly's house, I found myself once again keeping my pain bottled up within me. If Josephine didn't remember what had happened, I certainly didn't want to remind her of it.

From there my mind wandered to the awful nightmares I started having when I was four. Usually, they were of scary men climbing in our windows and taking us away, but I could vividly recall one even more terrifying. A huge spider—black with yellow polka dots—was attacking me in my bed. My screams woke Molly, who came in to check on me. But when I told her what happened, instead of comforting me she said, "Stop screaming and go back to sleep, there's nothing on your bed." The message was clear: I was not to wake Molly up again.

After she left I laid there in terror for what seemed like eternity before I finally fell asleep.

I started to feel like this woman didn't care about us as much as she said she did.

I was rarely sick as a child; in fact, other than two bouts of laryngitis, there was only one time I remember feeling ill. My stomach was churning, and I rushed to the bathroom, only to vomit in the hallway.

Once again, I called for Molly to come and help me, and was completely shocked when she said, "Since you made the mess, it's your job to clean it up."

I was still feeling queasy as I filled a bucket with water and grabbed a rag. After cleaning up the vomit I went and lay down. I didn't know what was worse—the sick feeling or how Molly had treated me.

Over the next year we stayed with Molly, all of us waiting for my father to be released from prison. Molly would tell me about the letters they wrote back and forth, and how she sent him secret messages by placing the stamp in a particular direction and/or location.

One time, she took me to the prison to see him. As she held me up to the window of the prison door, my eyes darted this way and that; I was so excited to see my father again. But I couldn't see clearly enough through the window to make out where he was, and I returned to the ground feeling cheated.

There was talk of him coming home and living with us again. I don't remember exactly when he got out of prison, but

I do remember that winter, when I was five years old, my dad and Molly got married.

In the days leading up to this event, I grew more and more excited. Finally, I thought, my sisters and I would have a mother to take care of us.

The special day turned out to be another disappointment, though. We all drove up to this huge building. The two of them got out of the car and went inside while we sat there in the freezing cold. I didn't understand; this was our family too, so why weren't we allowed in? Once again, it felt like the adults in our lives were rejecting us.

When Terrible Things Happen

Though the wedding had been a disappointment, I consoled myself with the fact that at least we now had a father and a mother under one roof. My father found himself a job and when he received his first paycheck he was so excited. He showed us what one hundred and fifty-dollar bills looked like. He seemed genuinely happy. Life was going to be good.

It didn't take long, though, for things to take a turn for the worse.

By now I was in first grade. One day we had an assembly at school about eating healthy foods. There was a lot of food there, and I made a comment to my teacher about not having a lot of food at home.

Though we didn't go hungry per se, money was an issue, which affected the amount and types of food we had. Molly had tried to arrange for others to live with us to help cover the rent, but it never worked out. Meals were therefore very simple and usually involved government-subsidized food. I remember we had lots of soup, including split pea, which I hated, rivel soup, which consisted mostly of milk and flour, and even "coffee soup" —which was just broken pieces of bread covered in coffee. (On occasion I still enjoy a bowl of coffee soup). There was also salmon soup, which I liked. We had Velveeta cheese and SPAM and flour gravy over toast. We also had dried milk to drink, which I despised. Whenever possible, we lived off the land, harvesting dandelions from the yard. (Later, my sister would tell me she recalled eating rabbit and squirrel stew and some kind of mush). One night I ate ten ears of corn for dinner, because that's all we had.

When I went to the assembly that day, I saw lots of different types of food that we never had at home. That was what I was thinking when I made the comment to my teacher. It seemed a harmless comment to me, so I was shocked when I walked home for lunch and was greeted by a very angry stepmother.

Molly grabbed hold of me, threw me in a chair at the table and started throwing food at me. It started with a peanut butter and jelly sandwich. "Make sure you eat every bite of food in front of you," she screamed, "You're not getting up from that chair until you're too stuffed to eat another bite!" Confused and terrified, I started to cry.

"Why would you tell someone that you don't have food at home to eat?" she demanded.

But I never said that, I thought to myself.

She then told me she'd gotten a call from my teacher. "If you ever say anything like that to anyone ever again, you'll wish that you hadn't."

By that time my lunch break was nearly over. I was afraid to return to school, but I was afraid to stay home too. I no longer felt safe anywhere. When I mustered up enough courage to go back, the teacher could tell something was wrong. She asked me if I was okay.

"I am fine." I replied, my stepmother's warning still ringing in my head. I couldn't imagine what would happen if I disobeyed her.

I got home that evening to find Molly had told my father about the food incident, and I got in trouble all over again.

Getting "in trouble" became a regular occurrence in our home. Josephine and I took most of the punishments, and though Heidi avoided a lot of the bad stuff, I now realize she was definitely affected by everything that happened. Shortly after school started, Molly gave birth to a baby, whom they named Alex. There must have been some complications with the pregnancy because I remember my father saying, "It's worth all the hassle, it's a boy." I never said anything to anyone about that comment, but I was crushed. *What's wrong with girls?* I thought to myself, *Why doesn't he like us?*

Now that baby Alex was in the picture the punishments seemed to become more severe. For even the smallest of offenses, we would be sent to the basement stoop. We had to stand inside the basement door with the lights out until they decided we could come back out. I never knew how long we were in there, but it always felt like forever. At first we begged and pleaded for them to let us out, but after a while we realized that once our eyes adjusted it wasn't so scary. It helped too when we could see the light under the crack of the door.

Eventually, my father and Molly caught on that we weren't crying as much, and because of this they moved on to more severe punishments. Now instead of standing on the basement stoop, we had to actually go down to the basement and into the coal bin. There was no light there whatsoever. Every time we were sent to the coal bin we were reminded that there were huge rats in there and we needed to be careful where we stood or they would get us. This was the real punishment—hearing every creaking noise and thinking it was the rats crawling around, waiting to pounce. Sometimes we stayed there for hours, to the point I would think they forgot we existed. I would stand as long as I could, then feeling my legs shaking with strain and fear, I would have to sit.

"Do you remember," Josephine said, pulling me out of that

coal bin and back to the present, "the time you threw a block at my head?"

I turned to my sister and nodded. We had been playing in the middle room of the home, where we had a few toys, including a set of wooden building blocks. I enjoyed building with them, and I was in the middle of my project when she took one from me. I responded by picking up another block and throwing it at her, hitting her in the head. It knocked her out. "Yes," I said, "I am so sorry I hurt you."

As we sat there in the car with our mother in front of Molly's old house, the conversation turned back to that middle room. I told her about the pirate's eye patch I'd had and how when it went missing I spent the entire day looking for it for fear of being punished.

I then asked her if any particular Christmas we'd spent there stood out in her mind.

"Yes," she replied, "I hated those bikes."

I nodded. "I was thinking the same thing."

It was our last Christmas in the house. Josephine and I had both gotten bikes, but they were too big for us; in fact, they were for adults, with twenty-six-inch tires. At just seven and eight years old, respectively, there was no way Josephine and I could ride them, so we were surprised when the weather got nicer and Dad and Molly put the bikes in the car and drove up to the top of a steep mountain. They put us on the bikes and said, "Now, ride it down the mountain."

Josephine and I looked at our father, then each other. We had never been on a bike in our lives and that mountain was a terrifying way to learn. I remember thinking, *What if we go over the edge?* There were no guardrails to catch us. Then I had an even scarier thought: *I wonder if he wants us to die.*

We didn't learn to ride that day, though Dad and Molly

certainly enjoyed themselves, laughing and urging us to just "get on the bikes and go." In fact, I don't remember ever learning to ride those bikes. I did just fine on a banana seat bike, but when my dad saw he said, "If you can ride that why can't you ride your own?" I didn't answer him, not knowing how to put into words the terror I felt when looking down that mountain. My feet hadn't even reached the pedals!

Our mother didn't say much, just listened as Josephine and I talked about this and other horrifying experiences. I got the distinct impression, which would be confirmed later, that Mom had not realized how bad things were for us while living with our father.

Finally I turned to Josephine and said, "I think it's time to move on."

She agreed, but as we drove through the alley alongside the house the memories continued to flash through my mind. We talked about our father's old pickup truck, and how he used to make us ride on a bench in the back. The bench wasn't attached, and we had to hold on tight because if we didn't the bench would fall over and we'd fall face first onto the steel bed. The worst was winter, when we had to ride back there even on the coldest of days. By the time we got where we were going our bodies would be chilled to the bone and our fingers aching terribly from hanging onto the bench.

There was one good thing I remembered about living in Molly's house: we started going to church. My dad had been introduced to church by his brother, my Uncle Sebastian, a kind man who lived about thirty minutes from us. I don't remember going on a regular basis but I do remember the occasional drive and sitting in Sunday School singing and learning about Bible stories. Our teacher used flannel graphs to show the actions of the characters. I felt safe there.

Last year I was puzzled when a woman named Cheryl reached out to me via Facebook. I could see from her profile that we had graduated from high school the same year, but I didn't remember having any classes with her; in fact, I didn't remember her at all. But curiosity got the better of me, and I sent her a message back. After a few friendly exchanges, we agreed to meet for lunch.

It was during the meal that Cheryl revealed that she was living in my old house. When I asked her how she knew where I had lived, she said she had done research on the place, including asking neighbors about previous residents.

As I listened to this, panic set in. Why would she keep that detail a secret until we met in person? Though I managed to keep my composure, Cheryl quickly realized I was not feeling comfortable at all.

Soon, however, it was her turn to be caught off-guard. I started describing the house to her in detail.

"How do you know all that?" she asked.

"Why do you ask?" I was a bit confused by the question. I had, after all, lived there.

"You just described my house from top to bottom."

"A lot of horrible things happened in that house," I replied, "When terrible things happen you don't ever forget."

In the course of our conversation, Cheryl revealed that her mother had worked at our elementary school and knew of my family—we were in fact one of two or three "troubled homes" in the community that the school was concerned about. She even knew about the "food incident." We later moved so she didn't know what had happened to us. This was very uncomfortable for me to hear, and I asked why she hadn't mentioned this when asking me to lunch, Cheryl said she thought I might not come. She was right, but she never apologized.

I left that lunch feeling very uncomfortable and, oddly, abused. Like I'd somehow been taken advantage of and needed to once again protect myself. I was thinking, How could I have let this happen?

As the unsettled feelings arose in the pit of my stomach, I became obsessed with the house. I wanted to go and pray over it. Despite Cheryl's trickery, I wanted her to be safe within the walls of that house, and though she felt safe I disagreed. Most of all, I wanted the memories to go away.

I started praying and asking God to help me be able to deal with all these fresh emotional wounds. Clearly, the house still had a stronghold on me and in order to move on with my life I needed to let it go.

God answered my prayers in the form of a healing prayer session at my church, through which I attained freedom from the inner turmoil the house represented.

With my eyes on Jesus, I no longer allow the house or the things that happened in that house to affect what is going on in my life today. The house nor the memories that came with it line up with what God tells us to dwell on.

Finally, brethren, whatever is true, whatever is honorable, whatever is right, whatever is pure, whatever is lovely, whatever is of good repute, if there is any excellence and if anything worthy of praise, dwell on these things.
~ Philippians 4:8 NAS

The Farm

The conversation was light as we headed back into the country toward our next location. Josephine and I weren't even sure we would be able to find the farm, where we had moved shortly before the flood, a deluge that washed out our outhouse and threatened the home itself. We had never returned since we moved from there, and our mother, who had never been there, had no idea where it was. We were determined to try anyway.

As we got closer things started to look familiar; when we saw the old school we knew we needed to make a turn, and we recognized the bridge, which had clearly been repaired since we lived there. Once we crossed the bridge and came to the stop sign I knew we were nearly there.

A few minutes later, we had arrived at the road leading to the farm. The landscape was a breathtaking vista of open fields, hills, and valleys. There were farms strewn here and there, and a narrow stream with cows grazing peacefully nearby. It all looked so perfect, I found it hard to believe we were in the right place. Yet in my heart I knew once we made that last turn it would only be seconds until we got to our old house.

We sat at the top of the hill for a while taking in the scenery; we even got out of the car and took pictures so we could remember the beauty of what lie in front of us. Josephine and I started talking about all the people who'd lived in the farms when we were growing up and what we remembered about each one of them.

As we looked down over the hill and behind the trees, we

could see it, our old farm. Something was different, though. The barn wasn't in the right place. The house looked different too, and where were all the sheds? This had to be the place, I told myself, it just had to be. Then my gaze landed on the pond, and just like that, the beauty we had been enjoying a moment earlier just seemed to evaporate.

Josephine and I decided it was time to take a closer look. As we got into the car, my heart started racing, then pounding in my chest. Even after everything we had endured today, coming here was even harder than I had imagined. I took a deep breath and reminded myself how close we were to finishing the journey.

We made that last turn down over the hill. As we approached the lane Josephine and I said, almost in unison, "There it is." It wasn't until we crossed over the creek and turned onto the lane that we realized how much things really had changed.

The old house we'd lived in was gone, replaced by a beautiful home. The garage was gone too, as were the tractor and saw dust sheds. The barn was no longer on the right side of the farm, and the hills where we'd kept the cows pastured were no longer the same. There were no more raspberry bushes or overgrown brush, and all the sumacs were gone around the burn pit. Even the lilac tree where I had buried our dog was now gone. Everything was different, manicured, cleaned up.

Obviously someone lived here. We decided to ask the new owner if we could take a look around. Mom and Josephine sat in the car while I went to knock on the door. It was answered by a very pleasant teenaged girl.

I asked if her parents were home and she went to get her mother. As the woman walked toward me my mind started racing and I wasn't sure what to say. *Get it together,* I told myself, *just calm down.*

Another deep breath and the words just spilled out. I introduced myself, explained that my sister and I had grown up in this house, or the house that used to be there, and would it be okay to take a look around? The woman, whose name was Sandy, said it was fine and to take as much time as we needed.

I thanked her, then turned back to the car and motioned for my mom and sister to get out. At first it seemed as though we were wandering around aimlessly because everything was different. Finally I just stopped and suggested we start from a spot that was still the same. That left us very few choices, two of which were the old oak tree and the creek behind the house. The tree sparked a memory of the poison oak I had gotten one year. It was no big deal, it just caused a lot of itching that sent me looking to the school nurse for relief.

From there, we started mapping the place in our memory. As we followed the path up from the old tree we figured out where the burn pit had to have been, which meant the house should have been across the lane from there. The new house was sitting where the garage used to be. My favorite maple tree was gone. The thought saddened me.

Then we remembered the two storage sheds and smokehouse, which we had always been forbidden to enter. Josephine asked if I knew why, and I explained that we rented the farm and the stuff in the sheds didn't belong to us. Not that we were ever tempted to go inside; we had looked in the windows and found the contents—mostly butchering supplies hanging from the ceiling—to be rather creepy.

As we talked I found myself growing upset that the house wasn't there; I'd hoped we would be able to go in and take a look around. Later, when I thought about it, I recognized this as a blessing, that going inside might have been too overwhelming. I thank God that He knows best what we can handle and what we can't.

We continued walking up the lane to what should have been the barn, but was now an open field. Then, as we passed the new barn, I realized even the milkweed was gone. How can everything just disappear? I didn't say anything to my mother or Josephine, I just kept trying to figure it out in my mind. I had buried another one of our dogs at the end of the milkweed patch, and now I had no idea where that might be.

As we moved past the spots where the tractor, sawdust, and water sheds used to be, Josephine recalled how she'd been responsible for taking care of the pheasants.

"What really happened with them?" I asked.

She said she didn't like taking care of them, so she simply stopped. As they started to die off, she threw them out back of the tractor shed. No one realized what was happening until we no longer had eggs to eat. Our father investigated, and though I don't remember the entire sequence of events I do know the outcome was not good for my sister. Memories, including that of the severe beating she took, started flooding my mind. I had nowhere to go to process or even think about all that had happened on this property. At that moment I just wanted to be able to climb up into my favorite maple tree and escape, but a glance at the spot where it once stood reminded me again that it too was gone.

How could this beautiful place still bring back such terrible memories? As I looked at the pond between the properties all I could think of was the day my cousin Eugene came to visit and asked me if I'd like to go fishing with him. I said, "Sure that will be fun." To my surprise he had other things in mind besides fishing.

At that time, I had no recollection of the earlier incident with me and Josephine. Unbeknownst to me, Eugene had gotten out of jail, saying he had changed, and apparently my father and stepmother believed him.

As we made our way across the little bridge and up the other side of the property we put the fishing gear down and we looked around the pond. He showed me all the tadpoles swimming along the edge of the pond. He explained to me how as they grew up they lost their tales and grew legs. We even tried to catch some. Then we picked up the gear and went to the far side of the pond.

We sat down on the ground with our backs facing the neighbors behind us. The trees to the right blocked the view of anyone in that direction. I was getting the fishing pole ready when he said, "No, I've changed my mind."

"But, I like fishing." I protested.

"I want to show you something…" He then unzipped his pants and said, "Can you kiss my friend?"

My heart began to race, and my mind right along with it. I thought of the neighbors and wondered if someone was going to help me, yet at the same time I was scared that they would help, for then my father would find out. If he did, I would surely get in trouble.

"I can't," I told Eugene.

He assured me it was okay, then he took hold of my head and placed it against his privates. Again he told me to kiss it. This time I did as he said.

I wanted to run and get as far away from him as possible. Why would he make me do this? It just didn't seem right.

Just then my sister made a comment about how beautiful the farm was now, once again pulling me back from the awful memory I was reliving.

I said nothing as we finished our journey around the farm and returned to the house. I knocked on the door again, this time to thank Sandy for her kindness.

Before I left, I asked, "Do you know what happened here, why everything is gone and the house and barn are all new?"

Sandy nodded. "Oh yes." She explained that the original owner sold the property to an Amish family, who moving in burned everything to the ground and rebuilt. I just stood there for a moment, unable to believe what I was hearing. *God is an awesome God,* I thought to myself.

For the next few minutes Sandy told me whatever she knew about the property, and I shared a few things about the various buildings that were once there.

"That explains some of the things we found in the old dump site out beyond the property," Sandy remarked.

"We used to take stuff out there," I said. "My father cut the top off an old car and we would fill it with our trash then take it to the dump site."

After thanking her again, we piled into the car, emotionally and physically spent. On the drive home we tried to process everything, all the while knowing it would take quite some time before we would be able to truly deal with the memories flooding our minds.

The Turning Point

I managed to hold it together until I had dropped off my mom and my sister, but once I arrived home the emotion erupted like a tidal wave. I literally cried until my eyes would no longer make tears. *What had I just done? What was I thinking? Why would I put myself through all that?* I didn't have answers to those questions, but I knew there had to be a purpose and I trusted God to let me know what it was on His time.

In the meantime, I felt like I had to do something, and the only thing I could think of was to write a letter. I sat down at my desk and soon found myself penning a note to Sandy. After thanking her yet again for her kindness, I explained a bit about the reasons we had gone there. I told her that not much good had happened while we lived on the farm, and how glad I was that everything had been burnt, for it meant no one would ever be hurt in the house or barn again. I told her I appreciated the opportunity to see it one last time, and even that my sister and I had talked about writing a book about our life growing up.

She replied with a kind, heartfelt letter that I didn't expect but became very precious to me.

> *Thank you for your kind letter. It is interesting to me to learn more about your family's time at this place...and clearly not all your memories are good ones.*
> *Our home is in Heaven! Thank God!*
> *No more crying there!*

You and your family will always be welcome here!
Please come back and spend some time with us.
May God bless you and heal all your memories!

In His love,
Sandy

Deeply moved, I tucked the letter away in my "treasure box," a small gold box that I'd had since I was in the hospital. The first items that went in the box were pictures I had drawn for my girls while I was there, to let them know I was okay. That box soon became a repository of memories for every step of the healing process. There are notes from other women who were with me at the hospital, as well as encouraging words from friends. Over the years other special notes and mementos would make their way into the box, and to this day I go through them every so often just to remind myself of how far I've come.

After our journey, Josephine and I indeed tried to write a book about our early experiences. Soon, though, painful, long-buried memories began to resurface, and with it, a great deal of stress and anxiety. As I mentioned earlier, everyone deals with trauma differently, and Josephine had done so by blocking many things from her mind. Heidi, our younger sister, had done the same thing; in fact, she remembered even less about our childhood than Josephine did.

I told Josephine that I only wanted to share things with her that she was ready to handle; I certainly didn't want to make an already painful experience even worse. Eventually, we decided to put the project on the back burner.

Even as I tried to help my sister process everything, things also started coming to the surface for me.

Those four years we spent on the farm had been the worst of our lives. For many years, I had managed to compartmentalize those memories in order to function, but our visit to the place had seemed to unleash something in me. I wasn't sure exactly what had happened, or why it seemed so much worse; I just knew the memories would not go away. Josephine and I started having regular late-night phone calls that lasted for hours. She remembered how when she did the dishes, if she didn't get them clean our father would make her eat out of the dog's dish. He would say something like, "This is what it feels like to eat out of dirty dishes." She said sometimes he would actually make her eat dog food. I hadn't remembered that, but she did.

Oddly enough, the turning point for my sister came not during one of our conversations, but while she was in a courtroom, offering moral support of a friend.

As soon as I answered her call I could tell something was wrong.

"I had an anxiety attack today," she said, "and I didn't know what to do."

When I asked her what happened, she told me about being in court but had to leave because of the attack. I asked her why and she started to cry. Apparently, she had had some sort of a vision but didn't fully understand it.

"I saw myself as a little girl wearing a red polka dot dress and my chest got tight and I couldn't breathe."

For a moment I froze, wondering how to best refresh her memory, then I reminded her of the picture of us in the polka dot dresses. She had said in the car that day that she remembered the picture, but it was black and white so she couldn't tell from it what color the dresses were.

I then gently walked her through that day in the courtroom, when we were four and five years old. The memory slowly came back and she was able to process it, but it didn't stop there. She continued to have other memories, which in turn led to more memories surfacing for me. It was as if we had tugged on a thread and were now unraveling the entire ugly fabric of our childhood.

Another day, our conversation led to the day she'd ended up with a swollen hand. I remembered that day all too well, though I did not know all the details.

She had done something our father did not approve of. He took her outside to the barn and when they returned her hand was the size of a softball.

I'd always been afraid to ask about that for fear something would happen to me. Now, finally, I summoned the courage to learn the truth.

"What really happened?" I asked, then felt sick when she told me how he'd taken her to the barn and made her punch him in the stomach over and over again until she couldn't move her hand at all.

When they came back into the house no one spoke about it. Dad and Molly wrapped her hand in gauze and the next day we were sent to school as if nothing happened. The school nurse disagreed, and when she saw the bandage around my sister's hand she called her into her office. She then unwrapped the gauze to see what was going on.

Shortly after, I too was summoned. When I got there, she told me that she'd examined my sister's hand and that Josephine told her what happened. She then asked me if I had been hurt in any way.

"No," I told her, "but there were other days that things had happened to me."

"Do you have any bruises on your body now?"

"I don't know," I said, and that's when she asked if she could take a look."

I had this sense of being scared and yet safe at the same time. Finally there was someone who seemed interested in what was going on with our lives. I allowed her to look at my back and arms because that's where most of my bruises would be if I had any.

The nurse documented the bruises she saw, then asked me how long this had been going on. I explained that it was all the time and we never knew when it's going to happen. She assured me that she would take care of it. I remember thinking, *finally we don't have to deal with this anymore.* What I didn't realize was what would happen next. Shortly after we visited the nurse's office, some people showed up at our home. It turned out they were from Child Protective Services. Later, when I looked back on that day, I would realize now that my dad and Molly had known they were coming.

We were clean and well-dressed when they arrived. The house had been cleaned and everything seemed fine.

As they visited we were told to go outside and play. When the meeting was almost over we were called back in. The women asked a few general questions and thanked us for talking with them. They did not, I remember, ask us any direct questions like the nurse had. Then, just as abruptly as they had shown up, they were heading out the door.

It seemed like only seconds later when my father called me into the kitchen. Honestly, I don't think they were even off our property yet, but I could tell from the way I was called that I was in trouble.

Immediately, my mind began to race as I tried to think of what I possibly could have done. I had no idea. Then he started yelling at me and asking why I would go to the school nurse. That's when the full impact of my mistake hit me. *But she had said she would take care of things...*

In that moment I realized no one was safe. No matter who I confided in, something always went wrong and I ended up in trouble.

My dad had the Wiffle ball bat in his hand. There was no escaping the wrath that was to come. I had to stand there and once again endure the pain of yet another beating.

That night, my sister and I talked about how we never knew when we were going to get beaten, or how even the smallest things set them off. Then our conversations took an even darker turn.

When some "transgression" occurred but the guilty party was not clear, our father would line us up and question us until someone confessed. Once this happened, the other two girls were then forced to beat the confessor with whatever belt, piece of wood, or other object he provided. Though we had no choice, these beatings eventually caused a rift between the three of us girls.

Of all the things Dad did to us, this may have been the vilest.

Fuzzy Bunny

Shortly after moving to the farm another baby, Aaron, entered our family.

To make room for our new brother we rearranged in the house and I ended up in a room by myself. I thought this was great—no more sharing a bed with my sisters. For the first time in my life, I would have some privacy.

On one occasion I was in my room, holding a small furry bunny someone had given me. I accidently rubbed it against something and a small piece of the fur came off. *That's interesting,* I thought as I continued picking the fur off, *I wonder what the bunny is actually made of* (it was my inquisitive mind, thinking again). A few minutes later, I held a naked pink plastic bunny that didn't look so pretty. Suddenly it occurred to me the trouble I would get into if Molly or my father discovered I had destroyed the toy. I looked around for a place to hide the evidence and finally put it under my bed. By the time I left my room, I had completely forgotten about it.

Later that week Molly called me to my room. As soon as I walked in I knew something was wrong but I had no idea what it was.

She called me over to the bed and asked, "What is it you do in this room when no one else is around?"

"Nothing," I replied, not sure what answer she was looking for.

"Let me refresh your memory." With that, she grabbed hold of my hair and yanked a hunk of it out of my head.

Hurting and confused, I started crying. I had no idea why she would do such a thing.

"Do you remember now?"

"No."

She repeated the action of pulling chunks of my hair out several more times, then asked again, do you remember now? I still had no answer to give her. Finally, she reached under my bed. When I saw her pull out the bald, pink bunny, I fell to the floor, not knowing what to do.

"While you're down there," she snapped, "clean up the hair and the mess you made and get rid of it all."

My head hurt so bad I just wanted to crawl in my bed and hide under the covers. Instead I did as she said, then headed outside, anything to get away from her.

There was a maple tree in the yard that had always looked so inviting. Now, my scalp still burning, I began to climb. I thought, *If I can get high enough no one will be able to find me. I can hide in the branches and be by myself.*

That tree became my sanctuary, a place where I could disappear from my world and the monsters in it. I even escaped my sisters because they were afraid to climb. Then one day my grandmother who now lived with us told Molly she had seen me climbing the tree. From that day on, it was forbidden.

Now, as an adult, I started to realize how things that happened in my childhood were still affecting my daily life; basically, I was still living in survival mode, as if the next traumatic experience was just around the corner.

One day, my sister-in-law Anna was visiting with her little girls. I watched as they played with her hair; they were making a mess of it.

"Why couldn't we ever do that to you?" My daughter Naomi asked.

I was taken aback by the question, but when I looked back at Anna and her girls I could barely stop myself from cringing. When they were young, my own daughters always wanted to brush my hair or play with it, but I always said no. Just the thought of it was unbearable. It was only now, after they were older and no longer interested, that I realized I had deprived them of something most little girls enjoy. If I wanted to move on, I needed to find a way to face what had happened.

I realized it had gotten out of hand one day when someone simply touched the tip of my hair and I swung my arm around and hit them to get them away from my head. My head was so sensitive that the slightest touch set me flying out of control. This kind of defensiveness made it very difficult to have friends. I didn't even let anyone cut my hair; I had learned to do that myself at the age of twelve.

A couple of years ago I was traveling with my youngest sister Emily and her friend Mary to a Joyce Meyer conference. I was sitting in the front seat and Emily was behind me. She accidently touched my hair and my body cringed as I jumped in my seat.

"What's wrong with you?" she asked.

That's when I finally told the story of what had happened to me.

Mary asked me, "How big is your God?"

"What! My God is big."

"He can't be too big," she replied, "if you let that bother you."

Puzzled, I asked what she meant by that.

Mary explained that just the day before Joyce Meyer had talked about how big God really is and that we make excuses not to allow Him to work in our lives. She used will power as an example and how people have a hard time controlling what they eat. She said if a person says they couldn't eat just one cookie they really have no self-control, but when we put our trust in God He can help us control that urge.

For the rest of the day I processed Mary's words, and how I wanted my God to be that big. Then I remembered the vision I had had back in the hospital years earlier and told myself my God is that BIG!

In the meantime, Emily had decided to test me and see how sensitive my head really was. Without warning, she would simply touch the tip of my hair and it would make me jump. Amazed, Emily said I needed to work on that. Every time she did it, the question, "How big is your God?" would pop into my mind.

I wish I could say I had a total breakthrough that day, but I didn't.

Shortly after that weekend I had an appointment with a new massage therapist. She asked me at the beginning of my appointment if I wanted a facial massage.

When I told her I'd never had one before she assured me they were very relaxing, so I agreed to it.

As she started our session I quickly realized it was not relaxing for me. As she massaged my face her fingers were going through my hair. Apparently she could feel me tensing up every time she did it because she asked if I was okay. I shared with her the story of what happened to me as a little girl but insisted it was time for me to get over it and move on in my life.

It was very difficult to lie there and allow her to continue. I just kept thinking I have a GREAT BIG God and with Him I can conquer anything.

I can do all things through Him who strengthens me.

~ Philippians 4:13 ESV

At the end of the massage session, she allowed me to give her a hug and I thanked her for her help in my recovery process.

When I look back on those days, I can't believe how bad I really was. The entire youth group at our church comments on it, and even some of the adults in our church talk about how no one could ever touch my hair.

Sometimes I'll walk up to a person that I once offended and say, "Go ahead touch my hair." Most times I get the same reaction—"No way!"—but I assure them I'm okay now. I can now have people touch my hair and my head with no reaction at all.

I say, Thank you God for Your amazing power.

Salvation

As time went by my chats with Josephine continued, though they seemed to grow fewer and farther between. One particular late-night conversation covered several topics ranging from how we used to labor in the fields and shuck corn in the barn to how we were both afraid to go in the watershed because of the snakes.

Corn shucking wasn't always bad, but there were lots of times when our hands were rubbed raw. Dad would always say, "The cows need to eat."

So do we, I'd think, though I never said it out loud. I knew better.

My sister and I talked about those really cold nights, and how we weren't allowed to come into the house until there was enough corn to feed the cows the next day.

I told about one bitterly cold winter evening when my hands were so cold I could no longer feel them. This of course made it even harder to shuck the corn, but finally I finished the task and headed to the house. It was pitch black outside, with only the faint glow from the kitchen window to guide my way.

I walked into the kitchen to find my dad and Molly sitting there. My two sisters were already in bed. My dad asked me what took so long, and I explained how cold it was and that I couldn't feel my fingers or toes.

Without a word my father got a bucket of water and placed my feet in them, then did the same for my hands. The water was cold, though, and I remember asking why I couldn't have warm water.

"If they are frostbitten," he replied, "warm water can cause more damage."

That didn't make sense to me but I had to take him at his word.

Sure enough, the feeling started to return to my toes and fingers.

"You'll be fine," he said, "now go to bed."

I headed off to my room, savoring the feeling of having my father care for me. It would go as quickly as it came.

As Josephine and I continued our conversation, we realized there never seemed to be a rhyme or reason to what happened on the farm.

We talked about all the bizarre punishments we would get and how they seemed like torture to us. We started to wonder if there might be some sort of a mental condition we didn't know about; one theory was that he had developed PTSD from serving in the army, but we couldn't be sure.

I asked her if she remembered the electric fence and some of the things that had happened.

"Yes, some."

She definitely remembered how scared we were of it.

Like many farms we had an electrified fence to keep livestock in and predators out. To stop the fence from short-circuiting, Josephine, Heidi, and I had to pull the grass around the cow pastures. The problem with doing that is on occasion our father would sneak to the barn and turn the fence on so we would be jolted if we accidently touched it. Since we never knew when this was going to happen, we always had to be on guard.

It seemed to take forever to pull all the grass and we wondered why we were never allowed to use the sickles.

"It's probably better we didn't," I remarked, "or we might

have been electrocuted."

She agreed.

Conversation then moved to how he punished us with the electric fence. Just the mention of it brought back horrible memories.

Like his "practical jokes," we never knew when this was going to happen; however, we always figured it out very quickly. First, Dad would take us on what seemed an eternal walk up the lane to the barn. Then we would be made to stand facing the fence.

It was the same every time. He would yell at us to grab the fence, and then use our tears to determine the length and severity of the punishment.

"The more you cry," he'd say, "the more you'll have to grab the fence."

Even as I write this, fear springs to my mind. Why would a father make his children do such a thing? Did he somehow get pleasure in seeing us hurt?

My heart breaks for him as I think of the torment he must live in day after day.

I told my sister about the time I went to the doctor for pain in my wrist. I was around twenty-two years old.

Thinking it might be carpal tunnel, the doctor sent me for testing. As they were running the tests, tears started to roll down my face. The nurse saw what was happening and asked me if it hurt that badly.

"No," I replied, "it was bringing back memories of how my father used to make us hold onto the electric fence for punishments."

Immediately she said we needed to stop.

"Is it done?" I asked.

"No, but the shock we send through the arm

intensifies as the test progresses and I don't want you to have to endure that pain again."

I thanked her for being so thoughtful and left the office.

Before we said goodnight, I asked my sister if we could try to end the conversation on a positive note, even though there wasn't much positive in our lives during those years.

I then told her about the one good memory I had at the farm. I wouldn't recall the circumstance leading up to it, just that one day my father was sitting in the chair in the living room and I crawled up on his lap and laid my head on his chest.

I remember hearing the sound of his heart beat and almost being scared by how loud it was. Yet, I didn't pull away because lying there on my father's chest brought me a rare feeling of peace.

It didn't last long. Molly came in and I had to get up. Yet I had never forgotten that moment, I told Josephine, and I would treasure it always.

When it was her turn, my sister couldn't really come up with a good memory.

"What about the times we got ice cream?"

Our father drove the church bus every Sunday, and during the summer months we would often stop for ice cream on the way home. That was a good time. She agreed she enjoyed that.

What was more important to me, though, was the time we spent at church.

We looked like a normal family, acted like a normal family and spoke to others rather freely while we were there. Then one night during a special service, something happened.

I felt the Lord speaking to my heart. I wanted to have the

Jesus they were talking about. I wanted to know He was part of my life. I was only nine years old but I knew that's what I wanted.

Even though we looked normal, my sisters and I knew not to leave our seats or move around; if we did we would be punished when we returned home. I sat there thinking, *How is this going to work?* As the evening started to wrap up, we got the hymnals out and opened to page three hundred. (Yes, I remember the page.) It was the song "Just As I Am". By the time we got to verse three,

> *Just as I am, though tossed about*
> *with many a conflict, many a doubt,*
> *fightings and fears within, without,*
> *O Lamb of God, I come, I come.*

I couldn't stand it any longer. I gently tapped on my father's arm and asked him if I could please go forward and pray for Jesus to come into my heart. To my amazement he said yes.

Before he could change his mind I quickly scooted out of the pew and headed for the front of the church. This was really happening! I was out of my father's reach and doing something on my own. It definitely felt right. One of the church elders came up to me as I knelt at the altar. She asked me if she could pray with me privately.

"Yes," I said, since I had never done this before. We went to a side room and spent some time talking and praying.

I felt new and refreshed, as if all life's burdens had been erased. I felt happy, so happy I wanted to tell the world about Jesus and how He can help you.

That night I felt an overwhelming sense of peace. I felt like everything was going to be alright.

The next week we once again headed to church. At the

closing of the service I was amazed again when my father leaned over and told my two sisters to go forward and ask Jesus into their hearts.

One Sunday shortly after this experience, the church was holding baptisms. Once again I asked if I could be part of it, and Dad agreed. He then told my sisters they were going to do it also.

They did as they were told, but afterward they both told me that it didn't really have much meaning for them. They didn't understand it. It wasn't until later in life that they realized the true meaning of having Jesus in their lives and came to a moment of Salvation.

I continue to pray for Josephine because I think she still struggles with having that personal relationship that goes along with having Jesus in our heart. At the same time I realize it is not my job to force anything on her and God will do His work when the time is right.

For He says, "At the acceptable time I listened to you, and on the day of Salvation I helped you. Behold, now is the acceptable time, behold now is the day of Salvation."
~ 2 Corinthians 6:2 NAS

Last Call

With such an awesome event taking place in my life I thought things would surely get better. Maybe the beatings and awful things would stop. Trust me when I say that did not happen. In fact, things went from bad to worse.

My last late-night call with Josephine was probably the hardest to deal with and probably the reason the calls ended. I can't say for sure, but maybe my sister just couldn't handle everything we discussed. What I do know is that somewhere during the call talk turned to what had happened at the top of the steps.

It was a bittersweet moment when I realized she too remembered those events. I was comforted that I was not alone in my memories but saddened that she carried the burden as well.

"If there was one word to describe our stepmother," she asked, "what would it be?"

"Evil and manipulative," I replied. "I know that's two words but that's how I feel." I then asked her, "What word would you use?"

"Evil is perfect," she said, then agreed that manipulative was equally appropriate.

Molly always had this way of twisting things to make us think we were the bad people or that one of us was better than the others.

She once told me that of the three girls I was the only one who would make something of her life. At the time I had such mixed emotions, I wasn't sure what to think or feel. It was her way of pitting us against each other.

She also knew how to drive a wedge between me and my father. I can't say for sure whether she also did this with my sisters, but I wouldn't be surprised.

One day, when I was about ten or eleven years old, she pulled me aside and asked me questions about my father and if he had ever touched me in an inappropriate way. It took me a few minutes to process what she was asking, then I told her that I honestly couldn't think of anything he had done wrong.

She proceeded to tell me that sometimes he felt things towards girls and that he acted upon those feelings. As if that wasn't enough, she then told me that he used to have an inappropriate relationship with his cousin.

I stood there thinking to myself, *Why are you telling me this? I don't want to hear about this stuff.* But the seed had been planted, and now I had this idea in my head that it wasn't safe to be around my own father.

It was this type of manipulation that led to the event at the top of the steps. To this day, my brain recoils from thinking about it and my heart breaks because of the evil Molly plunged us into that day.

When Molly called me and Josephine upstairs, we naturally assumed we had done something wrong and figured we were in for yet another beating. To our surprise she was very calm and started talking to us about growing up and what we could expect as we got older.

Then the conversation turned to boys and relationships. She explained that sometimes boys like to do certain things to girls to make them feel good. She began having the two of us experiment with each other. We didn't know what she was talking about and we apparently weren't doing things the right way because she said, "Let me show you."

That's when she crossed the line.

Josephine and I stood there, not realizing what was going on as she proceeded to sexually molest us. When she was done with her "demonstration" she asked, "Did it feel good?" What is a young child supposed to say to that? My body cringes at the memory of those words. I am filled with utter disgust that eats right through to the core of my being. I've always wondered how a woman could do such terrible things to the young children she is supposed to love and care for. And, though, I've experienced it firsthand it remains unimaginable to me.

I honestly don't even remember the rest of our conversation that evening. Maybe it was too much for me to handle also. What I do remember are the memories that flooded my being afterward.

Because we never discussed it further, I can't say for sure whether such a thing ever happened to Josephine again, but for me it didn't end there. I felt as though my stepmother was out to destroy my entire life.

Shortly after the event at the top of the stairs, Molly started taking me to our school bus driver's house. There didn't seem to be anything out of the ordinary. They would talk and then she would leave me to visit for a while. They had a huge latch hook on a loom in the living room, and the first several times he taught me how to do latch hook rugs and pillows. We would have lunch with his wife and there was always a snack, which was nice because we didn't get many snacks at home.

Then things changed. He would call and ask for me to come and visit. Molly would drop me off at his house. He too started sexually molesting me.

He was very bold about it. While his wife was in the kitchen cooking dinner, he would take me into the living room and sit me on his lap in front of the loom. There he would tell me to work on the latch hook as he proceeded to put his hands down my pants and fondle me, all the while talking to his wife as if nothing was happening. I couldn't even believe it was happening. I couldn't go home because it was too far away so I had to stay, trapped and helpless, until Molly came back to get me.

Then things escalated further. He got permission to keep me on the bus until the last stop, which meant he could abuse me more often. I dreaded riding the bus, and when there was no one else at my stop in the morning I would hide in the underground tunnel until I knew he drove past. Once he was gone I would come back out, walk home, and say I missed the bus.

This didn't go over very well with Molly because then she had to drive me to school. After school I would get a beating, but it was still better than having the bus driver's hands on me.

I never said anything to Molly about what went on in that house. She organized these "visits," and given her erratic and often horrific reactions to things, I was afraid to complain. Even worse, I realized I didn't have to tell her what the bus driver was doing to me, because she already knew.

Every time I returned home from the bus driver's house I had to take a bath. For most children bath time can be fun. For me, those bath nights were excruciating.

As the water was running, Molly would enter the bathroom with a scrub brush and a brown bottle of very pungent Lysol cleaner. She would then pour it into the bath, turning the water a pinkish red color. Then, as she stood there watching, I had to get into that foul-smelling water that made my skin feel like it was on fire.

Then she would tell me how dirty I was and make me scrub

my entire body with the Lysol and scrub brush. If she didn't think I was scrubbing hard enough she would tell me to scrub harder to make sure I got rid of all the filth.

I couldn't understand why she continued to allow me to go to the bus driver's house if she felt I was so dirty every time I came back from there. I certainly didn't want to go there.

I started to panic when it came time for my own children to go to school. How were they going to get there? The only option was for them to ride the bus. Well, that is just not going to happen, I told myself.

I would never allow my children to be put in harm's way. I understand now that my fears about them riding a bus stemmed from my own adolescence. To think that every bus driver was the same as my old bus driver was unfair. But in my mind all I could think of is there's no way they are riding a bus to school.

Even though we lived miles away from the school, every day I would put the girls in my car and make that trek to the school, home from the school, and back in the afternoon. At least I knew for sure my girls were safe.

In the midst of all that, my cousin Eugene came to live with us. Maybe it was because he had been caught before, but he had become very adept at sneaking up on me unnoticed.

One day I was in the barn taking care of the animal stalls when he slipped inside. I didn't even realize he was there because I was concentrating on getting my work done.

He approached me and said he'd be happy to clean out the stalls if I would help him with something. Of course I said, "Sure." Who wants to clean out smelly animal stalls if they don't have to?

A moment later, I quickly realized my mistake. Eugene forced me to have oral sex with him right there in the barn. *This is not worth it,* I thought to myself, *no matter how hard it is to clean the animal stalls.*

During the time he was with us he had a knack of catching me off guard and trapping me in places I couldn't get out of. I actually began to feel as though I was that filthy girl my stepmother kept telling me I was. There never seemed to be a way out or anyone to turn to for help.

The only thing I could do is ask God to help me through all that was happening to me.

We learned to pray while we were in church, so pray I did. I needed to somehow forgive these people who were hurting me but I couldn't figure out how to do it. All I knew is we learned that the Bible tells us to forgive many, many times. I just didn't feel like they deserved it.

The Visit

Once the school year ended things got a little easier. During the summer months my dad and Molly sometimes dropped us off at relatives so they could get a break. One time, my sisters and I found ourselves visiting our mother's parents.

For some reason I didn't really understand who they were. To me they were just an older couple we were visiting. I never recognized them as my grandparents until the day my mom unexpectedly returned to town.

"This is your mother, Rosie," I remember my grandmother saying, "and your sister Emily."

Suddenly, there were new possibilities and new people in our lives. Could it be true? Could things really change?

I very quickly attached myself to my mother. I wanted to be near her all the time. The first night she was there I was allowed to sleep in the same bed as her. I told her I wanted to sleep with her every night. She said she needed to let the other girls be with her also. I didn't see how that was fair. She was my mother. It never entered my mind that my sisters might want to be near her also. I never wanted her to leave me again.

I don't remember much about Emily on that visit. I do remember thinking she seemed a little bratty but hey, now I had three sisters. Maybe that would be fun.

To me, Mom was beautiful and I wanted to be with her forever. I spent every minute I could just watching everything she did. I watched her put on makeup. I watched her put curlers in her hair. This was peculiar to me because I had never seen curlers before that. When she took the curlers out of her hair it fell in long flowing waves. Yep, she was beautiful. She had this fancy mirror with lights around it that would change according to the setting you put it on. Everything she did was new and amazing to me.

After a few days of visiting, my mom told me she was going to be heading back to Cincinnati, where she now lived. Devastated, I clearly remember standing in the archway at the bottom of my grandparents' living room steps and begging her to take me with her. "I can't do that," she said, adding that she would if my father agreed to it but she knew he wouldn't. I didn't understand. I was sure he would allow me to go. After all, he really didn't seem to want me or my sisters around.

"If I can't go with you," I said, "can I at least have a picture to keep of you?"

Even after all these years, her words are so vivid in my mind, it's as if I am still standing there.

"No, if I give you a picture to take with you and your father finds it he will destroy it."

"I don't think he would do that," I said, then promised that if she gave me a picture I would keep it safe and not let him find it.

Just a short time later, she was gone. I didn't know if I would ever see her again, but at least I had the picture. I was so excited. I could always remember what she looked like.

A few days later my sisters and I went back home. I had placed the picture in a secure place; all I had to do was remember to get it as soon as we got in the house and then I could hide it. Nope, that's not what happened. The moment I tried to sneak it out of my belongings Molly asked me what I had. I told her it was nothing but she insisted on seeing it.

I gave her the picture. A few minutes later I was summoned

to the kitchen. My father sat there looking at the picture. He looked up at me and asked, "Why do you have this picture?" I told him the story of how my real mom showed up and said that if it was okay with him she would let me come live with her. Immediately Molly started talking about how I wouldn't be safe and how there are black people where she lives. She said the black people like little girls with blonde hair and if I went to live with my mother they would kidnap me and do horrible things to me.

Talk about fear setting in. The picture didn't seem important anymore. I didn't want to be kidnapped. I agreed to stay with my father and stepmother. I had never seen a black person in my life so I really wasn't sure what that all meant. I just knew it didn't sound good.

A very interesting thing happened just a few weeks later. My older sister went to live with my mom. She stayed home from school that day, supposedly because she was sick. When I came home she was gone. Just like that, gone. I didn't even get to say goodbye. I couldn't figure it out.

"Why is she allowed to go and not I?"

Molly and Dad told me she had wanted to go. When I asked about her being kidnapped, they replied, "She doesn't care about that and they wouldn't want her anyway."

It was all so confusing. My head was spinning.

I always wondered if I would ever see my sister again. Mostly I was concerned she would be kidnapped and have terrible things happen to her, even more terrible than what went on at the farm.

Torture

For a while after my sister left, things seemed to calm down. It didn't take long, though, until the rage started burning in my father and stepmother once again. I didn't understand any of it; all I knew was that life had become unbearable. It started with just beatings and gradually got worse. Each day hinged on my father's unpredictable moods. On one occasion, I came home from school with a permission slip for summer camp and handed it to my father. I never said he had to allow me to go, just that the school said he had to sign it.

In an instant he jumped up out of his seat, grabbed hold of my shoulders and threw me up against the basement door. I was completely stunned and speechless. I thought for sure I was going straight through the door and down the steps. Instead he just held me there. "Don't ever tell me I have to sign a paper again," he growled, "I don't have to do anything I don't want to do!"

"I'm sorry," I choked out through my tears. It was the only thing I could think of to say.

"I'll teach you how to show respect to adults," he said.

From that moment the rules changed to that of a military academy. We weren't allowed to speak unless spoken to or directly asked a question. When we responded it was, "Sir, yes sir, sir"; "No, sir"; or "Ma'am, yes, ma'am"; or "No, ma'am." Anything else led to swift, severe punishment.

This too drove a wedge between me and a sibling. My sister Heidi had always been a very timid and quiet child; now, if something went wrong, she would step up and say, "If no one else will, I will take the blame."

Eventually, I started to resent her, for this brave effort to protect us had the opposite effect. Every time she took the blame, she would immediately be let go and I would get punished once again.

Looking back, I believe that something was changing for my father during this time. Everything seemed to be more intense and more severe. One day when we were outside, my father took out his guns.

"I need something to use for target practice," he said to me, "I am going to give you a head start, you better run fast though because when I aim at you, you're going to want to be really far away."

I froze, terror filling my mind. What could I have possibly done to make him want to shoot me?

"Why are you still standing here?" he screamed, "Run, NOW!"

I took off as fast as I could. I just knew I was going to die. My dad did a lot of hunting and he always came home with animals. As I ran down the lane towards the road I heard several shots. With every shot I felt the little pebbles from our lane pelting the back of my legs.

I tried to run faster but my legs weren't cooperating. My mind, on the other hand, was racing frantically. *If I can get to the end of the lane and turn he won't be able to see me.* Then I thought, *Oh no, he's good at hunting, he'll run up over the hill and follow me down the other side.* Then I thought, *Why am I running? If he's going to kill me he's going to kill me!* As soon as that thought entered my mind, the shooting stopped and he yelled for me to get back to the house.

I couldn't believe it. I had survived. Why he stopped I will never know. What his purpose was, I will never know. What I do know is I feared for my life on a regular basis. Any sense of trust was completely gone.

To this day we have never had a gun in our house. I can't stand to look at them or even be around one. Once, Josephine came to visit with her boyfriend. He brought a gun with him to sell to Emily's husband. I was unaware that this was going to take place in my home. We were having a nice visit and Josephine's boyfriend went to the car to retrieve the gun so my brother-in-law could see it. He brought it in and laid the case on my dining room table. As soon as he opened the case and I saw what was in there I started to scream at him and told him to get that thing out of my house.

He thought I was kidding or something and started swinging it around. I yelled again and said, "GET IT OUT OF HERE!" He continued to ignore me. Then I slammed my hand down on the table and said, "Get out."

By then all eyes were on me, but I didn't care. I wanted no part of having a gun in my house, much less around my children. Finally, Emily stood up and said, "She said get it out of here, now do it."

The boyfriend mumbled, "What's the big deal, it's just a gun."

"I don't like guns," I said, "and I refuse to have them in my house."

Emily said, "It really doesn't matter why. It's her house and you should respect her wishes."

That's when I knew Emily truly cared about me. It was the one bright spot in a truly upsetting situation.

No doubt this reaction stemmed from what my father did

that day. When I think back on it I am reminded of the following Bible passage:

You fathers—if your children ask for a fish, do you give them a snake instead? Or if they ask for an egg, do you give them a scorpion? Of course not! So if you sinful people know how to give good gifts to your children, how much more will your heavenly Father give the Holy Spirit to those who ask Him? ~ Luke 11:11-13 NLT

Whenever I read this passage I think about my own father. Why wasn't he loving? Why did he give me a snake and a scorpion, instead of the fish and eggs? To these questions I will never have an answer.

As the days turned to months, to another year on the farm, fear became an ever-present part of my life. One particular day, Heidi and I were outside playing and actually having a pleasant time. Suddenly, Molly came out of the house and announced that Alex was missing. She couldn't find him anywhere, and no one knew how long he'd been gone.

My dad told us to split up and search for him. I was to go down the lane and search that area. When I didn't find him there I kept walking up the hill towards the bus stop. I couldn't imagine him going that far but since we couldn't be sure I kept looking. The road led back to another farmhouse, one I had never been to before.

I knocked on the door and when a gentleman answered I explained the situation and asked if he had seen my brother.

"No," he replied, "but if he comes this way I will call your father."

I thanked him and headed back home.

When I got back I went straight to my father to give him a

report. As soon as I saw him I could immediately tell the mood had changed.

"Where did you go?" he asked.

"To the farm up the hill, but I didn't find Alex."

I will never forget what he said next: "Do you know your brother could have drowned for all the time you were gone?"

"No, I thought someone else was checking down by the creek."

The next thing I knew he pulled me inside, where there stood a bucket of water. It wasn't a huge bucket but it was filled to the brim. My father told me to bend down and put my head over the bucket. Panic set in; now what? I shot a quick glance at my stepmother who was standing next to the bucket and knew she would be of no assistance to me.

"I want to show you what could have happened to your brother," my father said.

"So he's been found?"

"Yes," he replied, "no thanks to you. He was in the basement sleeping."

My flash of relief turned to terror as he grabbed my head and shoved it down in the bucket of water. It was so quick I didn't even have time to think or catch my breath. I struggled to get out but he held my head down. Just when I thought I couldn't hold my breath another second he pulled it up.

"Do you think your brother would have survived that if he fell in the creek?"

He then shoved my head in the bucket again, and again.

I was certain I wouldn't make it, certain today was the day I would die.

Then, as suddenly as it began, the punishment stopped. He pulled my head out of the water and simply said, "Go get yourself cleaned up."

Later that day, I went looking for my father to apologize for what I had done wrong. I couldn't find him or my stepmother, until I approached the basement door and heard talking. I opened the door and started to walk down the steps and I heard my stepmother say to my father, "You need to make a choice. It's either them or me. If I go I take the boys."

The next day instead of going to school we were told we were taking a trip. Molly put all our clothes in a laundry basket, some of them still damp from the washing machine. She piled me and Heidi into the car and off we went. I wondered where we were going. The ride seemed so long because no one was talking. Complete silence.

Finally, she pulled up to an unfamiliar, run-down house. I asked where we were, but she didn't answer at first, just got out of the car, unloaded the clothing onto the porch and told us to go inside.

"Who lives here?" I asked.

"This is your new home, your mother lives here." She then got back in the car and drove off, leaving us standing there on the porch.

I told Heidi to come with me and knocked on the door, but there was no answer. I tried the door knob and it was open. We entered the house and walked into the kitchen area.

"Mom..." I called out, but there was no answer. I walked into the dining room and called her again, still no answer.

I turned to Heidi. "Stay here. I'm going upstairs to see if anyone's home."

I called for my mom several times while heading up the steps. I couldn't figure out why our stepmother would drop us off at a house if no one was home. When I reached the top of the steps I called yet again.

This time I heard someone say, "Who's there?"

"It's me," I said, "your daughter." I then headed towards the voice and opened the bedroom door to find my mother in bed with a man I had never met before. "What are you doing here?" "We live here now." She was completely taken aback. "What do you mean, we live here now?" "Heidi is downstairs and we were dropped off and told this is our new home." I paused uncomfortably. "I thought you knew we were coming."

"No, I had no idea," she replied, then told me to go downstairs and she would be down to deal with the situation in a minute.

I did as she said and went downstairs. Despite my mother's reaction, I was thinking, *Thank you, Jesus, for getting us out of there!* Finally, no more beatings, no more electric fence, no more barn work or nasty bus drivers. I knew it probably wasn't the best way for a mother to find out she had two more children to take care of, but she was going to give it a try and I was thankful for that.

In this you greatly rejoice, even though now for a little while, if necessary, you have been distressed by various trials, so that the proof of your faith, being more precious than gold which is perishable, even though tested by fire, may be found to result in praise and glory and honor at the revelation of Jesus Christ; and though you have not seen Him, you love Him, and though you do not see Him now, but believe in Him, you greatly rejoice with joy inexpressible and full of glory, obtaining as the outcome of your faith the salvation of your souls. ~ 1 Peter 1: 6-9 NAS

Settling In

As my mom came down the steps, the strange man in tow, I remember thinking how beautiful she was. She introduced the man as her boyfriend, Gary. It felt a little awkward, but then the whole situation was a bit awkward so it didn't really matter. My mom asked if we were hungry. We said no we'd already had breakfast. Then she proceeded to go through the laundry that came with us.

We then got busy rearranging the bedrooms. Josephine, Heidi, and me took the master bedroom, and Mom moved into Josephine's old room. Emily kept the smallest bedroom. It seemed fair to me.

Josephine and Emily came home from school and we had a reunion of sorts. It was good to see that nothing bad had happened to Josephine, but it got me thinking. If it wasn't dangerous living with my mother in Cincinnati, I should have gone when Josephine did. Why, now that our mother had moved back to our local area, had they decided it was okay to live with her? After a while I dismissed the thought; I couldn't change the past, and besides, we were all together now. That was all that mattered.

Heidi and I were enrolled in school and life took on a rather normal routine. Each day, the three of us older girls walked to school together. I followed Josephine's lead and started forming friendships. This was new because while at the farm we never had friends come over and we were never allowed to go to anyone else's house either.

At first friends seemed to be a good thing. Most of the

friends I made were Josephine's friends because I followed her everywhere she went. The problem was I had this uncomfortable feeling most of the time that the things we were doing were not always good.

The one thing that really bothered me about moving in with my mom was the fact that she smoked. I could not stand the smell of it. Then one day my sister had some of her friends over to the house and they were all smoking too. They wanted me to join in but I said no. I told them that if they didn't stop I was going to tell my mom. That infuriated them all.

Suddenly, the oldest girl was demanding that I give her back the shirt I was wearing, which she had lent me. I told her I would give it back after I was done wearing it and it got washed. The next thing I knew, she was lunging at me. I took off out of the house and started running down the street. I got as far as the fire station when she caught me, beat me up, and ripped the shirt off me.

Luckily, my cousin Ben who lived nearby heard the commotion and came to see what was going on. He took me into his house and got me a blanket to cover myself. I couldn't figure out why the girl would do such a thing. Now the shirt wasn't good for anyone. It just didn't make sense.

That's when I realized Josephine had changed. Things were different now. We could never go back to the relation-ship we'd had before she left the farm. I didn't feel sorry for her anymore; I was too busy wondering how I was going to fit in. It was either join her crowd or find new friends altogether.

For a while I tried hanging out with her friends but it was never comfortable for me. I kept telling myself it was okay because I didn't know anyone else, but that all changed when the next school year started. Josephine and I were split up and put in opposite classes, so even though we were in the same grade we now had different teachers and different students in our classes.

I made new friends of my own, but though they were very nice and I had fun hanging out at their houses, something just didn't feel right. I had felt that way around Josephine's crowd, but this time it was different. This was about me, not fitting in. I felt as though they were too good for me to hang out with. They never said anything to that effect, but that's how I felt. And, since I didn't know what to do about it, I did nothing.

To make matters worse, Heidi was now hanging out with Josephine, which made me feel like an outcast in our house.

Emily proved to be a bit bothersome to me. There was something different about her. She was flighty and always getting into our stuff, and her room was always a mess. The novelty of having her as a sister wore off really quick.

My mom didn't really seem to have much time for us. When she was home she could usually be found sitting in the living room reading a book. Gary pretty much did the same thing. I really couldn't complain, though; books were a good thing, and a parent who read was certainly better than one who was always planning the next punishment.

We had food to eat and clothes on our back. We had a bed to sleep in, but something seemed to be missing. I just wasn't sure what that something was. It wasn't until many years later that I would realize it was love. There was no real love in our house.

We all had chores to do, which wouldn't have been so bad except that I always seemed to be grounded for one infraction or another, which meant I had to do the others' chores as well as my own. I started feeling like a real-life "Cinderella," and though I knew it wasn't nice I started thinking of Heidi, Josephine, and Emily as the wicked stepsisters.

What bothered me most about being grounded was that I was not allowed to attend church; it was the one thing Mom and Gary agreed on. I had found a nice church and looked forward to going every week. I also enjoyed Sunday school. I had become friends with a young boy and we sat next to each other. Honestly, we didn't pay much attention to what the teacher was saying, but we had fun.

I had also gotten involved with the church's midweek kids' program. I especially loved learning all the books in the Bible. One evening there was a competition to see who could say all the books from the Old and New Testament the fastest. Winning that was one of my proudest moments. I even won an award. It wasn't much, just a four-inch, glow-in-the-dark cross, but to me it might as well have been an Olympic gold medal. I kept the figurine for many years until sadly, it got lost in one of my many moves. The happy memory, however, will always live on in my mind.

For you are a holy people to the LORD your God; the LORD your God has chosen you to be a people for His own possession out of all the peoples who are on the face of the earth. The LORD did not set His love on you nor choose you because you were more in number than any of the peoples, for you were the fewest of all peoples, but because the LORD loved you and kept the oath which He swore to your forefathers, the LORD brought you out by a mighty hand and redeemed you... ~ Deuteronomy 7:6-8 NAS

Nightmare Relived

While living with my mother was certainly an improvement over the farm, things eventually started to feel *unsettled*. Gary seemed distant. It felt like we had become a burden. By that time I had made a small group of close friends, and I started spending more time away from home. I figured if I wasn't around I couldn't be blamed for anything.

One cool fall day I was walking home from a friend's when I saw a man and his wife walk out of their apartment and start putting laundry in their car. I noticed the woman seemed to be hurrying, but didn't think too much of it, given the chilly weather. Then I heard the man call my name.

I looked up and could not believe my eyes. There, standing just feet away from me, was my cousin Eugene. The same cousin who used to sneak up on me at the farm.

I froze for a minute, then managed a quiet, "Hi."

When he invited me inside to visit for a minute, I said, "No I have to get home."

"Come on, a few minutes won't hurt anything and my wife and son would like to meet you."

Everything in my body was telling me to go, but then I thought, *His wife and son are home. What could happen?*

"Okay," I said finally, "just a few minutes."

Once I got inside, he introduced us, then announced that his wife was taking their son to do laundry at her parents' house.

"Sit down," he added, "so we can catch up."

I shook my head. "No, I think I should go."

"Wait a minute until my wife gets her stuff and goes so

you're not in the way."

Once she was gone, though, he wouldn't let me leave. He shut the door and locked it and said, "Let's go talk."

I was trapped again. How did I fall for this? I just wanted to run but I couldn't get out.

He took a blanket and laid it on the floor in the middle of the living room. Then he asked me to join him. I pretended not to notice. The show "Emergency" was on TV and I acted as if I was really interested in what was happening. Then he called my name and pulled me to the floor.

When I asked him to stop, he said, "It's okay, you'll like this, it feels good."

"No," I said, "I want to go home."

He then proceeded to take my clothing off. I started screaming for help. But no one seemed to be outside and the window was closed, so I don't even know if anyone could hear me.

Once he finished undressing me, he told me to stop. When I didn't he put his hand over my mouth and held it as tight as he could. He placed his body on mine so I became trapped under his weight. I started hitting him and trying to get away. He grabbed my hands and held them over my head so I couldn't move.

At that moment I felt helpless. I closed my eyes and cried. I tried to focus on the TV show instead of him talking. I didn't want to hear anything he was saying. I was wishing that someone from the show could come and help me instead of the people they were helping on TV.

When he was through raping me, I got up and asked him where the bathroom was. He showed me and I went in the bathroom and tried to wash everything off. When I did there was blood and I cried some more. I thought he caused some internal injury or something. I was even more scared now. When I came out of the bathroom, I told him there was blood and he said, "Wait a minute."

I thought he was going to get me something to help me. Instead he came back with his son's piggy bank. He gave me a handful of dimes and nickels and said, "Don't tell anyone."

I didn't even know how to respond to that so I turned and left.

As I finished the walk to my house I became very aware of every move I made. What was going to happen to me now? I had to tell someone I was bleeding. I didn't want my outfit to get ruined from the blood. It was new. I especially liked my new top. It was olive green plaid with a half zipper front and brown patches on the elbows.

What would I do, what would I say? I couldn't keep it a secret; I might die.

When I walked into my house, my mom was sitting in the living room reading a book and Gary was in another chair reading his book. She looked up at me and I just remember saying, "Can I please talk to you upstairs?"

She shrugged in Gary's direction, then followed me. When we got upstairs I told her what happened and showed her the money Eugene had given me. I then told her I was really scared and that I needed to change.

"No," she said, "I need to get you to the hospital."

At the hospital, they tried to be nice but I didn't understand everything that was happening and it was all so uncomfortable. They asked me all kinds of questions. I felt like I was reliving it over again. When they were done doing what needed to be done, they decided to keep me overnight for observation. They didn't really explain the blood but said I would be okay.

As my girls Naomi and Elizabeth grew up, met their future husbands and became engaged, I told them I needed to have a talk with them.

I wanted them to be aware of what would happen when they consummated the marriage. I didn't want them to be scared like I was.

It was a very open conversation and I'm so glad we had the chance to discuss everything together. What I learned, though, is that I should have spoken with them sooner because they had both done their own research on the internet to find answers before I was brave enough to say anything.

It turned out to be a very lovely evening of women talking about everything that came to our minds.

We laughed a lot that evening as we talked about their lives growing up. They seemed to think that I make a great mom and I bring humor to their lives. What an honor.

This is my command—be strong and courageous! Do not be afraid or discouraged. For the LORD your God is with you wherever you go. ~ Joshua 1:9 NLT

The police showed up at the hospital and questioned me, then they took my clothing and the money that my cousin had given me. When I asked why they were taking everything, they replied, "We need it for evidence."

"But that's my new shirt."

They assured me I'd get it back some day. As for the money I was happy to give that up. I couldn't believe my cousin would take money from his own son and give it to me to be quiet.

I missed school the next day because I was still in the

hospital. But when I returned, I found out the story had been written up in the local paper. Everyone was talking about it. Though the article did not mention me by my name, I thought for sure my friends knew it was me.

Lunch was the worst. I sat there, trying to eat, while the conversation swirled around me. Everyone was trying to figure out who it was. What it must have been like. I just sat there in complete silence. If they didn't know I certainly was not going to be the one to tell them. I found myself withdrawing from them and I never went to their house again.

Later, I found out some of my friends did know, and they turned on me, saying things like, "Why did you do that to him, he's a nice guy?" and "Why did you tell such an awful lie?" I asked them how they even knew it was me. They said, "He's our friend and he told us you were trying to cause trouble for him."

After that, they never spoke to me again. I turned away from my other friends, because in my mind everyone would turn on me at some time or another. It was safer being by myself.

But that's not what God says.

Be strong and courageous. Do not be afraid or terrified because of them, for the LORD your God goes with you; He will never leave you nor forsake you. ~ *Deuteronomy 31:6 NIV*

The Gentleman

Things at home were also crumbling. Gary hadn't signed up for a woman with four girls living under her roof, and one day he decided he had enough. He packed up his stuff and left the house, never to return. Over the next couple of months there were other boyfriends, but no one ever stayed. I realized my mom knew a lot of men and I really didn't care for any of them. Until one day I came home to find a new friend at the house. His name was Lyle. He was different. He actually interacted with us. Lyle seemed interested in what we were doing and he talked to us. Or maybe it was just the way I personally felt, since no one else seems to have the same memories of this man.

I was twelve years old, and up to that point I had never met a man like him. Lyle was kind and showed me how to play a juice harp. He took the whole family on a trip to an amusement park. He bought us all gifts. When he left he promised to come back, but as time passed with no sign of him, I thought he was gone for good.

One day, I was walking down to my grandmother's when I saw this man was walking toward me. I looked and thought, *Could it be him?* I called his name, Lyle; no answer. I called his name again, and again I got no answer. But I was sure it was him, why wasn't he answering? Then, when we got about two feet apart, he picked me up and gave me the biggest hug I had ever had in my life. It was him! I forgot about going to my grandmother's. I turned around and skipped back to the house holding Lyles' hand.

We had a lovely visit that day but it ended way too soon.

When he was ready to leave he said it would probably be a very long time before he would be able to come back again. He said he would try, but I would be well into adulthood before I saw him again.

One day, Emily and I were talking when she suddenly asked me why my dad never came back. I asked her what she meant. Then I realized she didn't know who my dad was. She thought Lyle was my father. She said, "You've always talked about him as if he was your father so I just assumed he was."

That made me happy, just to be able to think about him again. But I wondered why he didn't come back.

I did a little research on the Internet and found out there were seven people in the United States with his name. I wrote a letter explaining who I was and why I was trying to find him and I sent a copy of it to everyone on that list.

I was so surprised when I actually received a phone call from Lyle. He said he would love to meet my new family and we arranged to meet at his house and then we went out for dinner.

When we arrived it was as if we had always been part of his family. He introduced us to his wife. I introduced Charlie and the girls to them, along with our sons John and Elijah.

His wife asked me why I was so fond of him. I explained how I grew up and although I had only met him twice he was the only man in my life that acted like a real gentleman. She was touched by the story. But they were both even more amazed to find out that I had named our oldest daughter after him. My husband and I agreed that her middle name would be the same as

his last name. If I'd had a boy, our son would have gotten his first name.
For years we stayed in touch, until he passed away.
I wish we would have had more time together.

There is a time for everything,
and a season for every activity under heaven:
a time to be born and a time to die,...
a time to weep and a time to laugh,
a time to mourn and a time to dance,
a time to scatter stones and a time to gather them,
a time to embrace and a time to refrain,
a time to search and a time to give up,
a time to keep and a time to throw away,
a time to tear and a time to mend,
a time to be silent and a time to speak,
a time to love and a time to hate,
a time for war and a time for peace...
He has made everything beautiful in its time.
~ Ecclesiastes 3:1-11 NIV

Justice is Served

After Lyle, I don't remember any other men coming to our house. However, during this time my mom started taking me to see a lawyer. I wasn't sure at first what was happening, but it became very clear, very quickly. What I had thought was behind me was now hitting me smack in the face again. I was now preparing for court. It was time to tell my story and hopefully do my part to make sure my cousin Eugene could never rape another person.

A person may think going to court is a frightening thing and I would agree it is, but what makes it even harder is when you have your own family members testifying against you.

The lawyer told me it was going to be hard and if I got scared to remember I never had to look at my cousin Eugene except if I was asked if I saw him in the courtroom. I told him I understood. He explained that the other lawyer would be asking me some really hard questions but I was to just tell the truth and if I couldn't handle it I was allowed to ask them to stop.

The day arrived and it was time to head to the courthouse. I don't remember feeling anything that day. It was like my body was almost robotic. I did what I needed to do.

As the lawyer had said, the questions were hard, but I told my story in as much detail as I could. Then they asked me questions about what I did when I got home. They asked me about what my mom was doing and where she was in the house. This made no sense to me, but I answered the questions truthfully just like the lawyer told me to. Once both sides were done questioning me they told me I could go out and wait in another chamber.

As I sat there waiting I started thinking about what I'd seen in the courtroom. My father was there. I hadn't seen him in such a long time. I was wondering why he was there and yet he wouldn't look at me or talk to me. It didn't make sense.

By the end of the day, my cousin was found guilty and sent to prison.

I thought the hard part was over until I asked my mom about my father and why he was there.

She said, "He was there to testify against you."

"Why would he do that?"

"They needed someone to prove that you were lying."

"But I wasn't," I said, completely aghast.

"I know."

"So what did he say?" I asked.

"He told them you lie all the time and can never be trusted."

My heart sank. *How could he say such a thing?*

"That's not the truth."

Then I was curious to know exactly what was said by everyone. Mom told me how my cousin had lied so much and got his story so mixed up that everyone knew he was lying. Then she told me I did a great job.

Our lawyer said the same when he came into the chambers to explain to everyone.

"All those details about what happened when you got home and how you remembered where your mom was sitting and that she was reading a book really clinched it."

I thought okay, I guess those questions weren't so stupid after all. I was glad I remembered.

To this day, what haunts me the most, aside from the rape itself, is that my own father testified against me. It breaks my heart that he would do that, and to think he thinks of me as a liar. There's nothing I can do to make him think differently.

One of the worst things for me is to have someone insinuate that I am not telling the truth. I become extremely defensive and want to prove to them that I am not lying. Most times it does not look pretty and it most always ends up in an argument. This is truly an area of weakness for me that I know God has shown me needs improvement.

As it states in *Proverbs 15:1-2 NIV:*

A gentle answer turns away wrath, but a harsh word stirs up anger. The tongue of the wise adorns knowledge, but the mouth of the fool gushes folly.

It's Not My Turn

Once all the court stuff was over life returned to "normal." With four children and a bartender's salary, it was hard for my mom to make ends meet. One day she brought Phyllis, a friend from work, home with her and explained that Phyllis was going to be staying with us. When my mom wasn't home she would act as a live-in sitter.

This was fine for the most part. Phyllis did make an occasional abrasive comment that made me uncomfortable, but I tried to ignore it. After all, it wasn't like I could make her leave.

Then came the big ordeal. One night, two weeks before Christmas, Phyllis told me to go out to the kitchen and do the dishes. My mother was at work.

"It's not my turn," I replied. I didn't usually talk back, but I was tired of doing everyone else's chores.

"I don't care whose turn it is," Phyllis said, "I told you to go out and do the dishes."

"No, I don't want to."

Her response changed my life forever. She got up out of her seat and grabbed me. I took off up the stairs, but she came after me and caught me by the hair. She threw me down the stairs and started beating on me.

Everything happened so fast I honestly didn't have time to react. I was in shock. Then she suddenly stopped, told me to stay put, then turned to my three sisters.

"Let's go, I'm taking you Christmas shopping for your mom."

As I lay there I thought, *Is that supposed to make me feel bad?* If so, it was the least of my concerns. My body was hurting so bad I was afraid to get up.

They all left and I inched my way down the remaining steps into the dining room. I thought, *Okay at least I am able to walk.* So I made my way to the kitchen and called the police.

When the police officer arrived he asked me what happened and I told him the story. He took a good look at me and saw I had blood on my face and my neck. He asked what happened there. I said, "I'm not exactly sure, but it was from what she had done to me."

He said, "I'd like to get you to the hospital and have them take a good look to make sure everything is okay."

I agreed, and he asked for my mom's information so he could contact her and let her know where I was and what had happened. I gave him the information but I never heard him call her.

After the hospital personnel cleaned me up and dressed the wounds they told me they were going to keep me overnight. I was more than willing to stay; I did not want to go back and have to deal with the situation at home again.

As I lay there in the hospital bed, I started wondering when my mom was going to get there. She never came. I realize now they probably told her not to come to protect me.

The next morning the officer came back to the hospital and said he needed to take me to the police station and meet with my mom. It was all so surreal.

The officer took me into a private room and told me he'd be back in a minute. When he returned he said, "Your mom is in another room. She is here to take you home."

I told him, "I don't want to go home with her unless she agrees to make Phyllis leave."

"Let me go see what I can do, I'll be right back."

When he returned he said, "Your mom is crying and she wants you to come home."

I thought for a moment, because I had never seen my mom cry. I asked the officer, "Is she willing to make Phyllis leave?"

He said, "No."

I said, "Then she really doesn't care and I cannot go with her."

"If you don't go with her then we will be forced to place you in foster care."

I said, "That's fine."

He left the room for a long period of time. As I sat there I started thinking. What is foster care? Where will I go? What does that mean? It didn't matter, I was tired of being beaten and unloved. In my mind anything had to be better than going back to where I came from.

I sat there for what seemed like forever, then the officer came back into the room and told me they had contacted my mother's brother and his wife, who were on their way.

"Why would they be coming?" I wondered how the officer had even known to contact my mother's brother, or, for that matter, that she even had a brother. Had my mother suggested this?

"They are coming to talk to you," he explained, "to see if it can be worked out that you might be able to go live with them."

"Okay, that would be nice."

He left the room again and promised to return when they arrived. In the meantime he arranged for me to get something to eat and drink since it was past lunchtime.

Later that afternoon, my aunt, uncle, and I had a nice conversation. I was glad they didn't ask about the details of what happened, though I imagined the officer had given them some information (years later I would learn that they actually knew nothing about my experiences, including the incident with the sitter). We discussed the possibility of me moving to their home and what I thought about sharing a room with their girls. I remember telling them I thought it would be fine since I had to share a room already with my sisters. They said they really wanted to try and make it work.

"There's just was one thing I'm worried about," I said.

"What is it?"

"My brother, Andy," I replied. "I know you adopted him. If *he* doesn't know and I let it slip that it would cause a problem."

By that time, he had been living with them for several years, and clearly my aunt and uncle thought I made a valid point, for they asked me to wait in the room while they went and discussed the matter further. The last thing any of us wanted was to cause Andy more turmoil.

When they returned to the room they told me they hadn't wanted to tell Andy yet but were now willing to do so. Considering the circumstances, they had little choice.

The Knife

It was decided I would be placed in foster care until Christmas vacation; this, so it would be easier to transition to a new school come January. In the interim Child Protective Services agreed they would take me back and forth to my current school.

That first evening at the Davises was frightening to say the least. When I arrived I was greeted by a George Davis and his wife, Pam, then I stood there while they spoke with Ellen, my caseworker. Once Ellen left they took me to the kitchen and gave me leftovers for dinner since they had already eaten.

After dinner we went to the living room, where three other teenagers—a girl and two boys—were sitting around watching TV. Everyone introduced themselves and we discussed the rules of the house.

Most of the rules were understandable—girls were not allowed in the boys' rooms and we were to show up promptly for mealtimes—but then the topic turned to showers. George told me the shower was set on a timer; if I wasn't done when the water turned off I'd be out of luck. I wasn't sure how long it took me to take a shower and just the thought of being left standing there with soap on my body or in my hair made me very nervous.

Aside from rushing through showers, the next week and a half was rather peaceful. Each day, I was driven to school by a social worker, and though the other kids seemed to know something had happened no one said anything to me about it. The worst part about it was that Josephine, who had stopped speaking to me since I left the home, was in some of the same classes. After school I was taken back to the Davis home, where I would hang out with the other foster kids. Then the day came for Christmas break. I said my goodbyes to the other kids and thanked George and Pam for giving me a place to stay, then gathered my belongings and hopped in Ellen's car.

When we got to my aunt and uncle's home, there was another exchange of pleasantries between them and Ellen, then, after wishing us all a Merry Christmas, Ellen took her leave. I couldn't believe I had finally arrived at my new home.

When they showed me to the room where I would be staying, I tried not to be disappointed. The room, which I was to share with their very young daughters, was small.

As I set my bag on the bed they had prepared for me, I decided I would make the best of it. Sure, it was not quite what I wanted, but at least I was safe and didn't have to worry about being hurt anymore.

Then I went to meet my brother or cousin, depending on how you view the situation. Andy, however, had no ambivalence about the situation. As we had discussed that day at the police station, my aunt and uncle had broken the news about him being my brother, and he was ecstatic.

He kept saying, "You are my sister," over and over, on a loop.

"Yes I am," I replied, smiling. It was impossible not to.

After a few days, however, it became uncomfortable, with Andy reminding me that we were brother and sister every chance he got. And each time, I would smile at him because I didn't know what else to say. I even started to wonder if I had made a mistake in asking my aunt and uncle to tell him the truth.

Though as an infant he had lived at Dad and Molly's, he was not their child but my mother's by some other man (we never learned his identity, just as Heidi and Emily never learned who their biological fathers were). From the day Andy was born my aunt and uncle had been willing to care for him; they knew my mother had already abandoned me and my sisters, and since my aunt's doctor told her she'd never have children of her own, she and my uncle had plenty of love and resources to give the new baby. They figured it was the best for all concerned.

For reasons known only to herself, my mother disagreed. She refused their offer, only to leave Andy in the care of my stepmother (my father was in prison at the time). Andy was a sickly baby and had many ear infections and repeated bouts of tonsillitis. Later, he experienced developmental delays in speech and walking. At some point my grandmother intervened, which led to my aunt and uncle officially adopting him.

Years later I found out that in fact he wasn't ready to handle this information. When I found out the impact it had on his life and what he went through to deal with the situation I was guilt-ridden. To this day I am amazed at how the choices we make in one situation affect the lives of so many other people around us, and how we may not even recognize the impact until long after.

I just ask that he be able to forgive me for my part in what took place and know that I love him no matter what.

Bear with each other and forgive one another if any of you has a grievance against someone. Forgive as the lord forgave you. And over all these virtues put on love, which binds them all together in perfect unity. Let the peace of Christ rule in your hearts, since as members of one body you were called to peace. And be thankful. ~ *Colossians 3:13-15 NIV*

Despite my initial discomfort, I did start spending time with Andy, trying to get to know him better. He also had cool toys and model airplanes, and we'd often hang in his room, playing with them. I was not as kind to the girls, who were much younger than me and far less interesting, but on the whole, living there was not unpleasant. Then, just a few days after Christmas, the relative peacefulness of my aunt and uncle's home completely shattered.

It started with a letter I had written to the teens at the Davis home. In that original draft I'd stated, "It stinks here." I didn't mean any harm, just that there wasn't much to do. We lived in the country, with a huge yard, but no neighbors and none of the activities I was used to living at my mom's house in town. In any event, when I read through the letter I decided I would rewrite it. The original was thrown away and quickly forgotten.

Then one evening a knock at the door startled me. When my aunt opened the door my heart sank and my mind started to race. What in the world were my father and Molly doing here? How did they even know I was here? Immediately I felt unsafe and wanted to run and hide.

At first it didn't seem like they were even interested in me. They came in, sat down and started talking with my aunt and uncle. After a few minutes I decided it was okay to leave and headed back to my room. It was safer there.

I wasn't there long, though, when my aunt called me back out to the living room. Now I was scared. Had they decided they no longer wanted me there? Was I going back to live with my father? I so did not even want to think about that, and as I sat there in the chair I remember just staring off into space trying to disconnect myself from the conversation that was going on around me. Suddenly, my aunt got up and went to the kitchen, where she took a knife from the drawer. She then walked back to the living room and threw the knife on the TV tray next to my chair.

I was so startled I jumped up and looked at the knife as if it was going to stab me.

"If you're going to kill me," my aunt said, "kill me now!"

I stared up at her, completely confused.

"Why would you write such horrible things in a letter?" she asked.

I still had no idea what she was talking about, until she pulled a piece of paper from her pocket. It took me a minute to realize it was the draft of my letter, which she had retrieved from the trash.

At that moment Molly chimed in. "Why don't you read it to her?"

My aunt unfolded the paper and read, "It stinks here."

My heart sank. Though to me they didn't seem like words meant to kill anyone, she was clearly deeply offended by them. I admitted to writing the letter and tried to explain, but again Molly chimed in and said, "Apparently she doesn't appreciate anything good when it's offered to her."

At that moment I felt as though I had just been stabbed in the heart. It was a note, and a discarded one at that, written by a lonely teenager with no friends and no one my age to talk to. It didn't mean I wasn't grateful that they had given me a place to live.

No one ever asked me about my feelings, though; they just told me to leave the room, which I gladly did, those familiar feelings of not being safe rising within me. What would happen to me now? Was I going to be sent back to my father's?

The visit ended and nothing changed for a while, except now I felt like my aunt no longer cared for me. It hurt, deeply.

Sure enough, a few months later, Ellen showed up to move me to a new home that according to her would be "better suited for me."

"For I know the plans I have for you," declares the LORD, "plans to prosper you and not to harm you, plans to give you hope and a future." ~ Jeremiah 29:11 NIV

The Walk

As we drove to this new home, I wondered what the people would be like and whether there were any other children living there. As if reading my thoughts, Ellen started telling me about the couple and how they had no kids of their own. She then said something puzzling: that there were currently no other foster children there either, which might be better since "I struggled having other children around me."

Why would she say that? I thought about asking her, but I didn't. Maybe it would be okay not having other kids around. It might be peaceful. At least I wouldn't have to share a room with anyone.

After what seemed like a long drive we finally pulled up to the house. I was intrigued by the fact that this new family lived on a street that was named after them. I wasn't sure, but it sounded like they must be pretty important.

The woman, Claire, was in the kitchen making potato rolls. Her husband was not home from work yet, but she said he would be home soon. Ellen didn't stick around long, and when she left Claire showed me to my room, then where the bathroom and the linens were. All of the rooms seemed so big, and the thought of having space all to myself was looking better than ever. She left me to settle in and said I could come downstairs whenever I was ready.

I remember sitting on the double bed and thinking, I wonder how long I'm supposed to stay up here before I join her. So I just sat there taking in my new surroundings and feeling uncertain as to what I was expected to do next. I needed to make this work so they wouldn't move me again. I decided to lie down on the bed. As I laid there thinking I thought about the size of the bed. I'd never had a bed this big to myself. The room was filled with sunlight shining through the three windows. It felt nice. I could look out the windows and see the garage and the smaller, matching house on their property. I wondered who lived there and if they were nice. I wondered if they had any kids my age to hang out with.

Then I heard the man come home. I stayed in my room for a while as I heard them talking. I was sure they were discussing me but tried not to eavesdrop. That would be rude.

After a short while Claire called me down and said it was time to wash up for dinner. Now, this was a new concept to me. Why should I wash up? I hadn't done anything to be dirty, but I went to the bathroom and washed my hands anyway before going downstairs.

As I walked through the living room I took a better look around. It was very nice. There was another room off to the left that didn't seem like it got used much at all. I thought it might be pretty nice being here. I'd just have to figure out the rules and what is expected of me.

I entered the kitchen to find Claire and her husband, Fred, already sitting at the table. I took my seat and we started eating. Those potato rolls were delicious. I had never really learned about cooking. No one ever seemed interested in teaching me. But I asked her if she would show me how to make them.

She said, "The next time I make them I'll let you help."

I thanked her, and we spent the rest of the meal making small talk. I learned that Fred enjoyed woodworking and fishing and Claire didn't seem to do much except stay home and take care of the house. I also learned that Fred's elderly mother lived in the little house next to them. She couldn't get around on her own and having her close made it easier for them to look after her. Though I was disappointed that there was no one for me to hang out with, I was encouraged by the fact that Fred and Claire were kind enough to help her out. I got settled in and started school. Everything seemed okay. Fred allowed me to use his fishing poles, and I would walk along the path behind their home that led to a creek. I found a nice big tree that had a place to sit in the center of the roots where I could hang my feet over the edge of the creek and fish. It was peaceful there and I didn't have a care in the world except how many fish I would be able to catch. It really wasn't hard because the fish hung out under the roots that protruded from the tree. All I had to do is put the line in the water and let it dangle there. I got a bite every time.

On other days Fred would allow me to watch him in his wood shop. It was fascinating to me. He would take a piece of wood and place it on a lathe and before you knew it he had created a chair leg or some fancy piece of wood that he needed to fix something in the house.

Claire wasn't as friendly as Fred, and I didn't have as much interaction with her. She would let me sit in the room off the side of the living room and listen to music with her. I remember going through her records and listening to John Denver. I thought it was the coolest thing to be able to have a room just to listen to music. I also went with her to her mother-in-law's house and watched as she fixed the bed or dusted the room. She would take meals for her every day. I especially liked watching her fix the old woman's hair.

Once in a while Claire would ask me to take a meal over. Fred's mother and I would chat, and sometimes she asked me to fix her chair or something. Life seemed pretty good. I was liking my new home.

I also started to make friends, and though I didn't get to see them much outside of school, it didn't seem to matter. Life was pretty peaceful. I was introduced to opera and musical plays. At first I thought it was boring, but then I started looking forward to the next time.

Before I knew it, spring had arrived, and with it warm days that were perfect for taking walks. I realized the dirt road that was named after them wound around and came back out to the main road further up the road. There was a little country store there, and I started stopping in and talking to the owner. She told me that a lot of the teens that lived with Fred and Claire would stop by and get snacks and stuff. This was great news to me. I found a new sense of freedom.

During one of my walks I ran into Wes, a friend from school. I had no idea he lived so close, let alone along the path that I regularly walked on. I told Wes where I lived and we talked for a short time and then I headed back to the house.

The next day there was a knock on the door. I was feeling comfortable in the Johnson's home so I decided it was okay for me to answer. I pulled it open and was surprised to see Wes had come to visit.

I was even more surprised by Claire's reaction. She accused me of inviting him to come without their permission. I tried to assure her I'd had no idea he was coming, but she didn't believe me. This was never to happen again; in fact, she said I had to tell Wes he couldn't come over anymore. This wasn't too big of a deal to me, I just couldn't understand why she didn't believe me.

Shortly after this I decided to go for a walk again along the same dirt road. I didn't stop or visit anyone, I just walked. What I didn't know was this was one of those nights Claire and Fred had planned on going to an opera. By the time I got back Claire was extremely upset that she missed the show. I apologized but it didn't seem to matter. She said they came out looking for me and wanted to know where I was. I told her I was walking around the dirt road. Again she said I was lying and that I had to have gone to somebody's house. I told her I didn't. I still am not sure how they could have missed me if they drove around looking for me because I never left the dirt road but she insisted they did and I couldn't convince her otherwise.

This event led to a break in the relationship. She no longer wanted me in their home. She said I couldn't be trusted.

Before long Ellen once again showed up to collect me and my bags. I was moving on yet again.

A few years ago I ran into Fred and Claire at the local hospital. I sat there for a while just trying to figure out for sure if it was them or not. I decided to go over and say hi.

As we talked she said she didn't actually remember me but that they loved doing foster care except for the last couple of teens they had. She went on to say they were awful.

I offered my apologies for the struggles they'd had, then, after offering my prayers for the dialysis treatment Fred was having, I said my goodbyes. As I left it all came back and I wondered what I had done that was so awful. See, I was the last foster child they took in to their home.

All I could think of is God tells us to love everyone.

When I heard that Fred had passed away, I sent a card.

Dear friends, let us love one another, for love comes from God. Everyone who loves has been born of God and knows God. Whoever does not love does not know God, because God is love. ~ 1 John 4:7-8 NIV

The Pool

As we traveled down the road to the new home I'd be staying in, Ellen explained that there were no children in this home either but Stella's granddaughter stayed with her on occasion. I listened as she talked but didn't really respond. I thought to myself, what does that matter to me? It's not like I had a choice in the situation. I was surprised that the new home was only minutes away. This meant that I'd at least be staying in the same school district. I figured that was a good thing.

As we pulled into the driveway I saw two new homes side by side with a two-car garage sitting in the middle. There was no grass, only dirt and stones. I thought, *How peculiar not to have grass in your yard.* I found out that Stella's husband had recently passed away and she'd used her inheritance to build two new homes, one for herself and her two adult sons that lived with her and the other for her daughter and her husband, who lived next door.

As I walked inside, I assessed yet another set of new surroundings. It seemed like a nice enough home. It was a split level with three bedrooms upstairs and a pool hall downstairs with a bedroom off to the side. There was another room where they hung out and watched TV.

Living there was a rather strange experience. I had a roof over my head and given access to food and a shower; I never really felt connected to the family. Stella never seemed to leave her room, and I rarely saw her sons, Ben and Phil. They were at work all day and spent their evenings hanging out in their rooms or in the TV room. Vicki, Stella's granddaughter turned out to be extremely annoying, and I made every attempt to hide from her, usually under the steps. Stella's home was a split-level, and one of the staircases had a huge, open L-shaped space under it. At the opening there was a door that opened into a coat closet. I would crawl under the coats and back into the L of the steps area, which I made into my own little room, decorating it with blankets and books. When the door was closed, Vicki couldn't see me because of the coats hanging there. I had even figured out how to lock the door so she couldn't get it open. For a while it was my treasured refuge, but before long I was told I couldn't lock her out of this space.

It became my responsibility to clean the house and do the laundry. I was used to doing these things so it wasn't odd to me but for some reason it didn't seem right that there were three adults just lying around.

Shortly after moving in I was introduced to the neighbors down the lane. Their daughter Jill was in the same grade as me. There was also another family up the lane with children, and though they were younger than me I sometimes went and rode horses with them. I spent more time, though, down the lane at my new friend Jill's house. As this relationship grew it started to change. It was the first time I was introduced to drugs.

One day, when her mom was in another part of the house, Jill got a baggie with pills in it from her pocket. She showed me them, explaining that the pink ones were called "Pinky Ds," the blue ones were called "Robin Eggs" and the black ones were called "Black Beauties." She asked me if I wanted to try one.

"Why would I want to do that?" I asked.

"Because they make you feel good," she replied.

"How do you know?"

"Because I've tried them already," she said, adding, "They don't hurt you and they don't really do much but make you feel relaxed."

I stared at the pills and decided I didn't want to mess around with something I knew nothing about. The first chance I got I excused myself and headed back to Stella's.

On another occasion Jill asked me to go fishing with her and her grandfather. Thinking it would be fun, I got Stella's permission and headed over there.

As we drove to the spot where we were going fishing Jill asked me to sit in the middle of the truck so she could sit by the window.

I didn't want to sit in the middle but I said okay.

This fishing experience turned out a little different than I expected. We all went down to the creek. Her grandfather took the poles and bait. Jill and I waded in the water for a while since it was a shallow creek. Then her grandfather called us over.

He asked if I had ever tried fly-fishing.

I told him, "No."

"Want to give it a try?"

"Sure."

About this time my friend started to wander off. She didn't seem interested in fishing at all, and I wondered why she had even come here. It didn't matter, though, just like it didn't matter that I wasn't very good at fly-fishing. I was just enjoying the new experience.

The same couldn't be said of her grandfather, who seemed frustrated that I kept getting the line stuck in the trees. After a while he suggested I go find Jill, which I did.

Later, as we drove home, I reflected on the pleasant day we'd had. When we got to Jill's house, I went to follow her out of the truck, but her grandfather told me to stay, that he would take me home.

I told him I was fine walking, but he insisted. He started backing out of their driveway but once Jill disappeared into the house he stopped the truck.

"What's wrong?" I asked.

"Nothing, I just thought we could get to know each other better." Then he started to rub my leg with his hand. This was not a good feeling. Immediately I wanted out.

"No," I said, "I don't want to."

"But didn't you have fun today?"

I told him I had.

"Then don't you think we could get to know each other better?"

"No," I said, my hand already on the door handle. I opened it and hopped out. "I'm going to walk home."

I shut the door and started walking, as he pulled the truck back in their driveway. I was scared that something was going to happen, or that he would say something to Stella.

I never went back to Jill's house. She would ask but I kept making excuses. I don't think anything was ever said and as far as I know no one spoke of the incident until now.

Summer came and another girl came to live at Stella's. Penny seemed nice enough. It took a couple days for her to settle in and get used to her new surroundings, but once she did we hit it off. We played pool and listened to music together; we even made up our own dances to certain songs.

Things got even better when Stella had an in-ground pool installed. Penny and I spent lots of our time swimming and splashing around. The kids from up the lane came, and we had such a good time I didn't even mind that Vicki was there. One day, Vicki and Tanya, the neighbor girl, were playing together. I was lounging in the pool and Peter the neighbor boy was messing around. Then we all started playing together, trying to see who could hold their breath the longest. When I saw that Peter didn't seem to be able to stay under very long, I thought I would try to help him. As he went under I placed my hands on his head and held him down. He started to squirm and I kept holding him. I figured he could last a little longer. Well, when he came up he was crying. He ran home and told his mother I had tried to drown him. Of course this wasn't the case, but I could see how it would seem like it to a young boy. It must have seemed this way to Stella too, because she reported the incident to Ellen and before I knew it I was being removed from the home.

Being shuffled from place to place never got easy, but after so many times I had almost become numb to it. But something about this was different. I wasn't taking all my belongings with me, just some of my clothing and my toiletries which I placed next to me in the backseat of Ellen's car.

Usually, as Ellen drove, she would tell me a bit about the people I would be staying with; this time, all she said was that she'd never been to the place she was taking me, but it was a long drive and I should sit back and relax.

I didn't know what to say to that, so I didn't say anything. How could she be taking me somewhere she had never been? It just didn't make sense. I tried to fall asleep but that wasn't happening. My stomach was is knots and all I could think was, *When is this ride going to be over?* The further we drove the sicker I felt.

I still felt as though God would protect me, but something

had changed. He didn't seem as close anymore. Yet I still remembered His words:

So do not fear, for I am with you; do not be dismayed, for I am your God. I will strengthen you and help you; I will uphold you with my righteous right hand. ~ Isaiah 41:10 NIV

Have I not commanded you? Be strong and courageous. Do not be afraid; do not be discouraged, for the LORD your God will be with you wherever you go. ~ Joshua 1:9 NIV

These words were my only comfort as Ellen's car sped to my new home, wherever and whatever it may be.

Juvenile Prison

After four long hours, we finally arrived. I stared at the place in shock, for in all my imaginings about what the place would be like, none had even been close. We were not pulling up to a house, but a *facility*. Where had Ellen taken me? When we walked in I was informed that I would be staying there for thirty days, after which they would determine what to do with me. Staff members escorted me to a dismal room with grey cement brick walls, two twin beds, and two dressers. My suitcase was placed on one of the beds, then, after telling me to wait there, they left, closing the door behind them.

I looked around the room, truly scared. There were no mirrors or personal items, and the windows were different than any I had ever seen. They had wire in the glass and bars on the outside. I had no idea what to expect and I couldn't imagine why they brought me here. What did they mean by "we will determine what to do with you?"

Obviously I'm going back to foster care. Half my clothes are still at the foster home.

But even as I told myself this, I realized I didn't believe it.

Then it dawned on me: I must be in juvenile prison.

Anger filled me. How could Peter get me in trouble like this? He had to have known I wasn't trying to hurt him.

The longer I sat there waiting for someone to return the angrier I got. *Okay,* I thought, trying to calm myself, *I have to make the best of this. I have to figure out how to get out of here.*

Finally, one of the staff returned. Her name was Heather.

She opened my suitcase and started rummaging through my belongings.

I was appalled. "Why are you doing that?"

"I'm searching for drugs and drug paraphernalia."

"I don't do drugs, and there's nothing in there."

"That's what everyone says."

I didn't say anything else but my mind was racing. *Wow, how dare she think I could be doing drugs? Who is she to be going through my stuff?* Then it hit me how completely powerless I was. I had been powerless plenty of times, but this was different.

She finally finished her search, then sat me down on the bed and started to explain the rules. As she spoke, I found myself wishing I was back at the Davis' house, where all I had to worry about was a shower with a timer.

"You will not be allowed out of this room for the next three days," she said. "Today the door will be kept shut and you cannot have any visitors. We will bring you your dinner, and you'll eat it in here by yourself. If you have to go to the bathroom one of the staff will take you."

She said all this in a maddeningly matter-of-fact tone. "Tomorrow the door will be opened and people may greet you at your door, but you may not talk to anyone and you may not leave the room."

I looked at her, my head spinning. What would make my caseworker think I needed to be placed here?

If Heather could tell how shaken I was she gave no indication. "Provided you do okay on the second day, on the third day the door will remain open, and you will be able to speak to the other kids. Then, on the fourth day, you will be allowed out of the room to eat and do activities with them."

Yay for me.

"You'll be able to smoke only in the lounge area and once a week we do a dresser search to see who keeps their clothes nicely arranged in their drawers. The person with the nicest drawers receives a soda or a candy bar."

She then asked me if I had any questions.

"No," I said, "and I don't smoke."

"That's fine," she said, then she left the room.

I know how to keep my drawers neat, I thought, *Maybe I'll get a soda or candy bar. That's something to look forward to.* I later learned that these inspections were less about neatness and more about making sure no one had snuck in drugs or other contraband.

After putting my clothes away I did as Heather had said. I sat in my room doing nothing.

On the second day it was strange having people walk by and stare at you but not be able to speak to them. The third day wasn't too bad. I still couldn't leave the room, but several kids came by to introduce themselves, which was very intimidating but better than being isolated in my room. One girl whose name I don't remember stayed to play cards, and she warned me that another girl hadn't liked the way I looked at her and I should be careful when I got out of the room. This was scary, but fortunately the girl would be removed from the facility before I had a chance to meet her.

For the next twenty-seven days I attended school in the basement of the building. I had people watching every move I made. I had doctors talking to me and asking me all kinds of questions. They did an IQ test and apparently they were quite impressed with my results, telling me that at fourteen, I had a college-level vocabulary. I thought, *Great what good does that do me in this place?*

Our daily schedule included time for relaxation techniques.

All of us were told to lie on the floor, side by side, in the hallway. After starting off with some deep breathing, we were guided to focus on every breath and imagine all our muscles were relaxing and that the stress was leaving our bodies through our hands and feet. We were then told to imagine being somewhere peaceful. They always wanted us to go to the ocean or on a beach, but this didn't work for me. I had never been to a beach and thinking about the ocean brought up a tarrying memory of my father throwing me in the creek. Instead, I usually tried to go to a meadow—a huge open area of grass surrounded by trees. All the forest animals would come out to play in the meadow and I would sit there watching them. It was my happy place that didn't exist anywhere else.

There was just one rule at relaxation time: we could not touch each other. I didn't think much of it until I met Wally.

By the time he got there I had been at the facility a while. The first thing I noticed about him was his unruly, wiry hair, but we soon developed a strong emotional bond that today is much clearer to me than his appearance. We had similar stories, and as we shared them I realized for the first time in my life I felt understood.

Each day at relaxation Wally and I made sure to lay next to each other, and in a spot far from Dave, the instructor. During the process we'd gradually get closer and closer until we were able to hold hands. We thought we were pulling a fast one, until one day Dave decided to walk back and forth. As he got close to us he reiterated the no-touching rule and we realized we'd been caught. No one made a big ordeal about it, though, so I guess they weren't too upset about it.

As Heather had said that first day, there were weekly room and dresser checks. While the rest of us were at school, the staff would pick one teen to help them with the inspections.

Week after week, my dresser and room were determined to be the cleanest and I was awarded a six-pack of soda. Then one week something changed and I didn't get the soda. I couldn't understand. No one's dresser was ever as neat as mine.

Sure enough, when I got back to my room and opened my drawers I found them in complete disarray. I was devastated, not because I hadn't won but because someone had deliberately sabotaged me. Obviously they were upset about me getting all the soda.

Every evening we had quiet time, when everyone went to their rooms to read or write letters or do homework. One night, just before lights out, I heard a loud noise, followed by footsteps and yelling. Everyone rushed to their doors to see what was happening. It turns out one of the girls in the room across the hall was upset about something and tried to escape by breaking her window and jumping. In doing so she got her arm caught in the window because of the metal that was between the layers of glass.

She was rushed to the hospital and the counselors rushed the rest of us into the lounge area. Once everyone was in there they started passing out cigarettes. When they got to me, I shook my head. "I don't smoke."

"Take one anyway," the counselor said, "It will help you calm down."

I took the cigarette, all the while thinking it was ridiculous. First, they couldn't have been observing me very well if they thought I smoked. Second, I wasn't even upset by what had happened. I lit the cigarettes and inhaled; it would be the first of many to follow.

At first I didn't understand the counselors' logic, but then I overheard them talking. They didn't want anyone else to try anything and figured if we were all in the same room they would have better control of the situation. It all seemed crazy to me. Eventually we were allowed to return to our rooms. Shortly after this incident it was time for me to be released from the facility. That day I sat at the counselor's desk waiting while they finished my paperwork. The soda machine vendor showed up to refill the soda machine and collected the money. I watched him for a while, then got bored and asked if I could return to my room and finish packing.

"Sure," Heather said, "I have to sign off on this stuff anyway and it will take me a while."

I returned to my room, finished packing and then sat there and waited. It seemed like forever before Heather came in. Finally, I thought, *Finally I'll get out of here.* But instead of telling me to come with her, Heather opened my suitcase and started going through it.

"What are you doing?" I asked incredulously, "I just packed that."

"I know. And I need to look for some missing items."

"I didn't take anything."

She informed me that some of the money from the soda machine was missing, and since I was sitting at the desk while the vendor was counting money, they needed to make sure it wasn't me.

Again I insisted I didn't take anything.

Heather didn't respond to that, but the next thing I knew she was asking me to remove my clothing.

"WHAT?"

"This calls for a strip search."

I couldn't believe it. Why wouldn't she believe me? I wasn't a thief.

"I'm not sure what a strip search is."

She told me again to remove all of my clothing.

"Everything?"

"Yes, everything."

Horrified, I began taking off my clothes. "Could I have some privacy?"

"No I have to watch to make sure you don't hide the money some place."

Again I told her, "I didn't take the money."

"It has to be you," she replied, "You were the only other person out there during that time."

Someone is setting me up, I thought. For all I knew it had been the vendor himself! But of course I couldn't say that. So there I stood, removing my clothing, already feeling disgraced, as if I'd been convicted of the crime. I certainly did not feel close to God anymore.

When I was naked, Heather swiftly conducted her strip search and of course found nothing.

"You can get dressed now."

"Now what?" I asked.

"I'm not sure, because we have to find the money."

"Well, I don't have it and I don't know where it is."

"Okay," she said, but she didn't sound convinced. Then she left the room.

As I write this I am overwhelmed with all the information that had been locked away in my head, all but forgotten, until I started to put my thoughts down on paper.

The human mind is an amazing thing; in order to protect us it files away information until we are able to handle it.

That's when God says, "Okay, it's time for you to be healed."

The information then slowly comes to the surface so we can face it, deal with it and get rid of it. We still have the memories but they can no longer hurt us or keep us stuck in dysfunctional, destructive patterns.

I originally thought this section of the book would be about two or three chapters; however, I now realize that the writing itself is part of an ongoing healing process. I may not have felt close to God during this time of my life, but I now understand that He never left my side—I was just unable to see or feel His presence because of all the trauma I had endured. Today, I know He is with me now and always and that I am protected from any harm.

I am reminded once again as the scripture says:

Finally, brothers and sisters, whatever is true, whatever is noble, whatever is right, whatever is pure, whatever is lovely, whatever is admirable—if anything is excellent or praiseworthy—think about such things. ~ Philippians 4:8 NIV

During those dark times we need to find something—even if it's just one thing—that fits one of these descriptions and hold onto it. Meditate on it day and night. Because no matter what ugliness is going on around us God is always there. Always.

Finally, be strong in the Lord and in His mighty power. Put on the full armor of God, so that you can take your stand against the devil's schemes. For our struggle is not against flesh and blood, but against the rulers, against the authorities, against the powers of this dark world and against the spiritual forces of evil in the heavenly realms. Therefore put on the full armor of God, so that when the day of evil comes, you may be able to stand your ground, and after you have done everything, to stand. Stand firm then, with the belt of truth buckled around your waist, with the breastplate of righteousness in place, and with your feet fitted with the readiness that comes from the gospel of peace. In addition to all this, take up the shield of faith, with which you can extinguish all the flaming arrows of the evil one. Take the helmet of salvation and the sword of the Spirit, which is the word of God. ~ *Ephesians 6:10-17 NIV*

Reunited

Finally, the day came for me to be released from the facility. I never thought I'd be so happy to see Ellen, or for that long drive. I was excited and, after what had happened, rather surprised to be going back to Stella Petrova's home. I figured I'd pick up where I left off at school and spend my spare time hanging out with Penny.

That illusion soon faded, however, when I got to the house and sensed a palpable tension. Everyone in the house seemed to be on edge, but I decided I'd do my best to ignore it.

As I went downstairs to the poolroom I was surprised to see there was yet another girl living in this home. I was even more surprised when I learned she was also named Penny! How confusing is that?! When Stella called out the name did they both come running?

This tension only seemed to grow as time went on. The new Penny and I did not get along, and the old Penny no longer wanted to hang out with me. By then I was old news.

Things were often different at school. Kate, my closest friend, now seemed distant and I could not figure out why.

One day I finally pulled her aside. "Why don't you hang out with me anymore?"

"I'm not allowed to."

Stunned, I asked, "What, why not?"

"My mom says when a person is in foster care, they are a troubled teen."

In just a few short months, I had been labeled an attempted killer, a thief and a "troubled teen." It was just too much to bear.

I asked her to give me a chance. I explained that I was in foster care because my parents didn't care about me. Kate held her ground. "My mom says I can't hang out with you or be your friend."

In that moment, I realized I couldn't trust anyone. I would have to figure out how to do life on my own. It was all about protecting myself.

Angry and saddened by Kate's abandonment, I turned my attention to Scott, a guy who had shown some interest in me. I started walking the halls each morning looking for him, and one day my efforts paid off. We started talking on a regular basis and he asked me to the Christmas dance. I told him I'd have to ask for permission. After all, it's not like I could just go home and say, "Hey, Mom and Dad, will you go buy me a dress?"

When I got back to Stella's that day I asked her if I could go. She in turn contacted Ellen, who said it was indeed okay.

To my surprise, this seemed to lighten the tension in the house, at least for a while. I was taken to the Salvation Army, where we found a light green chiffon dress that fit nicely. I couldn't believe this was happening. I was actually going to a school dance!

That night, Scott came to the house to pick me up. He exchanged pleasantries with the family and presented me with a very pretty corsage made of holly. I had never felt so special.

When we arrived at the dance, that feeling quickly shifted from "special" to "different." The first thing I noticed was my dress was outdated compared to those the other girls were wearing. No one said anything, but I felt it keenly. My discomfort increased when Scott and I joined a table of his friends. As we sat there, talking politely, all I could think of were all the labels that had been placed on me. If anyone found out, I just knew I would not be accepted.

It was a relief when Scott took me out on the dance floor, that is, until it dawned on me that I had no idea how to dance. Scott was very nice about it, and he showed me the best he could what to do. It wasn't until he took me home that I was finally able to reflect on how well the night had gone.

Our relationship continued for a short time, then one day he told me he was breaking it off to go back with his old girlfriend. My hurt over this got much worse when I learned he had just been using me to make her jealous. Though Scott had not been outwardly cruel to me, I felt abused and alone all over again. I tried to tell myself there was nothing I could do and there was no sense in fretting about it, but it felt lousy all the same.

Now I had no friends and no boyfriends, and though things were still tense at home I think Stella felt sorry for me. When her daughter told her of someone who had puppies and was trying to find homes for them, it was decided I could get a dog.

She took me to see the puppies, and they were so cute we ended up taking two, who we named Sugar and Sheba. I kept Sugar, and Sheba went home with her daughter.

Sugar became my best friend. Wherever I went she went. Then one day, as I was sitting in the TV room Sugar went into convulsions. Thinking she may have gotten into poison or something we rushed her to the vet, but the test results revealed that she had had a seizure.

I was told that if it ever happened again I had to make sure I kept her tongue from going down her throat. This scared me.

I was on constant watch. For a while everything seemed to be okay, then one day it happened again. This time they took her to the vet and the vet prescribed medication.

As Ben brought her in the house after the vet visit, he said to me, "We are going to have to make some tough decisions."

"What do you mean?" I asked.

He proceeded to tell me they could not afford the medication, which meant I couldn't keep her.

"No," I exclaimed, "that's not fair!"

He told me, "If we allow her to continue like this she will just suffer."

I looked at Sugar and back at him and knew I would never see her again.

That day he took her to the woods, where he put her down and disposed of her body. I was crushed.

Shortly after that, we were getting ready for school one day when the newer Penny started arguing with me. I no longer remember what it was about, but I do recall that it hit me the wrong way.

I grabbed hold of her shirt, lifted her off the floor and smashed her up against the wall.

"Don't you ever talk to me that way again!"

I then put her back down, let go of her shirt, and headed out the door.

When I returned home later that day, I found my suitcase packed and Ellen waiting to take me to yet another home.

As we walked out I realized I was glad. At least this time I knew why I was leaving. Maybe a fresh start would make things better.

While at Stella's I had also discovered that no matter what my other labels suggested, I was nothing if not a survivor, able to adapt to most any situation. And that was exactly what

I was about to do.

By this time, my mind was not focused on God. I didn't even go to church anymore.

About two years ago, as I was going through a time of searching and healing, I remembered Kate and how nice she'd been to me before her mom said she couldn't be my friend.

Low and behold, I was able to find her via Facebook. After telling her who I was, I explained the impact she'd had on my life, just by being a friend during that time in my life. I then asked if she would be willing to meet with me. I was a bit taken aback when she replied that she didn't remember me but was willing to have dinner. I was even more surprised when she asked me to meet her on her birthday!

I said, "Absolutely."

That night, we spent several hours exchanging life stories, and what I learned truly shocked me. The girl who had portrayed herself as a happy teenager, had actually had a terrible childhood. I had never noticed it because I was so absorbed in what was happening to me.

When asked about her birthday and why she would want to spend it with someone she didn't even remember she said, "I choose whom I want to spend my days with and at this time in my life I choose to be reconnected with an old friend."

I was so touched by her words and realized we really can't judge someone by their appearances. We really need to build those relationships and get to know each other. We need to pray for one another and share one another's burdens.

Therefore, as God's chosen people, holy and dearly loved, clothe yourselves with compassion, kindness, humility, gentleness, and patience. Bear with each other and forgive one another if any of you has a grievance against someone. Forgive as the Lord forgave you. And over all these virtues put on love, which binds them all together in perfect unity.

~ Colossians 3:12-14 NIV

Living With a Real Family

Though I was somewhat relieved to be leaving Stella's house, I couldn't help but wonder what lie ahead of me now. One's imagination can really go wild if they let it! As Ellen's car sped along toward my uncertain future, I realized that no matter where I had been and what I had been through, I could never really be prepared.

The drive was pleasant, and not as long as some of the others. For some reason, I found that comforting. When we arrived at the house, I grabbed my suitcase out of the backseat of the car and followed Ellen to the door. The problem was she wasn't sure which door to use—the one at front of the house or another on the side by the driveway. Just then the side door opened to reveal a friendly-looking woman. She introduced herself as Joyce Greene.

"Come in," she said, waving us in, "We're just about to eat dinner."

When we went in, I noticed a man and four children— two teenage girls and two younger boys—sitting at the table. I don't remember what Ellen did—she probably just observed as I was introduced to everyone. There was Ken, Joyce's husband, their daughter Gretchen, and another girl, Diane, who was also in foster care. Both girls were in high school. The two boys, Zach and Seth, were Joyce and Ken's sons.

As soon as I took a seat at the table, they said grace. It was like nothing I'd had ever heard before, yet they were all saying it in unison.

What is this?

When grace was finished Joyce must have noticed my look of confusion because she said to me, "I'm sure you'll pick it up quickly, and then you can join us if you'd like." As I had at my other foster homes, I tried to my best to settle into the routine. The Greene's were Catholic, and as Catholics they prayed the same prayer at every meal. As Joyce predicted I learned the prayer rather quickly and was soon saying it along with the family.

After dinner one evening, Joyce and I chatted as we put the dishes in the dishwasher. It was the perfect opportunity to bring up something that had been on my mind, but I wasn't sure how to approach her. After a few minutes of hemming and hawing, I finally just came out with it.

"What would you like me to call you while I'm here?"

"You're welcome to call us by our first names," she replied, "or you can call us Mom and Dad."

I was completely taken aback by this. "Really?"

"Absolutely, most foster kids who stay with us prefer that."

"Okay," I said, "I'll think about it."

At first, it seemed so strange to call someone other than your biological parents Mom and Dad, but the more I thought about it and the longer I lived there, it felt like a real home and a real family, so I thought, *Why not?*

The Greenes owned a coat factory with a store attached, and after school the boys and I would walk into town and meet Mom and Dad there. If they weren't finished working we were allowed to go to the stream and feed the ducks. I enjoyed feeding the ducks but I wasn't too keen on all the duck poo lying scattered around on the grass we walked in.

As fall turned to winter, they took me to their store and told me to pick out any coat I wanted. After looking around, I chose a brown coat with a large checked pattern and a black fur collar. I thought I was pretty cool walking around in my new coat, but I never told anyone how I felt because they might think I was weird. How could I explain that it was the first new coat I could remember having, that this gift made me feel as though they really cared about me? Their daughter Gretchen was forever sewing something or creating some kind of quilt, and she inspired me to learn to sew as well. I took Home Ec. in school and, sure enough, I loved it. At first I was making aprons with the rest of the class, but then I went on to make two dresses, one blue and other brown, each with a matching plaid vest. They were all interchangeable. After that I made my first lined wool coat. The teacher not only gave me an A, she said she'd never had a student take on such an ambitious project. I was thrilled that I had accomplished such a task. I would wear that coat for years, finally retiring it when I was in my early twenties and it was threadbare.

Life at the Greene's was pleasant. I shared a room with Diane, but she eventually left after getting in trouble with the law. After that, I had a room to myself, a rare privilege I wholly appreciated.

We did things as a family, including going to Seth and Zach's baseball and basketball games. The basketball games were particularly enjoyable—I was amazed watching these tiny little boys running around the court trying to make a basket. Mom once made a comment that the basket should be lower so they could actually score more points. Baseball was also fun because it was outside and you could walk around and hang out with friends.

We also attended church each week, and though it was a Catholic church I felt at home there. I connected with the people, and more importantly, I felt connected to God again.

For a time I even considered becoming Catholic, even if I didn't agree with everything they did, like eating certain foods on Friday or praying to Mary.

Zach had a newspaper route, and after school I helped him deliver his papers. We would race to see who would get their part done the quickest. He took more papers than I did because he had a bike and I had to walk. He usually ended up back home before me.

School was going well for me. The students accepted me as just another new student. No one seemed to know that I was in a foster home and I preferred to leave it like that. I decided to go out for track and field but quickly learned that I did not care to run.

The guidance counselor at school must have heard something about me, though, because one day she called me into her office and told me she had spoken to Mom and Ellen.

"There's something different about you," she said, "and I think you have great potential."

This was news to me. "What do you mean by 'something different'?"

"I mean you're different than most foster children I meet," she replied.

"Thank you," I said, not sure how else to respond. The only other foster children I'd met were in the homes I'd been in, and they didn't seem all that different from me.

The counselor then asked if I was interested in getting a job. When I told her I would like that, she seemed pleased. She said she knew of a place that was hiring and if I went and put an application in she would recommend me for the job. She wanted to help me, she said.

The job turned out to be at the local hoagie shop. I went there and put in my application, and true to her word, the counselor gave me a personal recommendation. Before I knew it I was busy making sandwiches and pizza and earning my own money for the first time. Mom showed her support by opening a savings account for me and I started regularly depositing some of my earnings. It was nice to finally have something of my own, and to know that the adults in my life believed in me.

When my birthday came around, Mom and Dad bought me a bike. I treasured the gift, and the freedom it afforded me. I rode that bike everywhere.

They also introduced me to roller skating. At first I was so nervous, I just watched the others laughing and smiling as they went round and round. It looked like a lot of fun, but I had no idea what to do. After a while I slowly made my way out on to the rink and was thrilled one of the people who worked there remarked that I was "doing a great job" and was a "natural."

I was making friends. I would go to their homes or they would come to mine. It was like being a real teenager with a real family. At some point, Albert, another teenager, came to stay. He too seemed to fit in and everyone got along well.

One night Mom and Dad received a phone call and we were informed that yet another teenage boy would be joining us for a short time. Everyone was curious what he would be like.

When he arrived, guitar slung over his shoulder, I couldn't help but stare at him. He was cute, as well as intriguing. I'd never known any foster kid with their own guitar. That night, while everyone else was downstairs, he and I sat upstairs in the living room and I asked him if he would play it for me. He played music I had never heard before, then he sang me a song called "Operator." I sat there, mesmerized. I felt so special, like he was serenading me. The next day he left and I never saw him again.

One evening about three months after coming to the Greenes' I was out in the neighborhood collecting money for Zach's paper route. I went from door to door and was surprised when Connor, a boy I recognized from school, answered. I didn't know him, but his parents were close friends with Mom and Dad. We struck up a conversation that night, and eventually started dating. I didn't really know much about having a boyfriend, but it was nice for a while. We took walks together, went to football games and the boys' baseball and basketball games, and hung out at the local pool. But after a while I started feeling uncomfortable. Connor showed me love that I had never experienced before and, frankly, found hard to accept. Deciding he was being "too clingy," I broke it off one day during lunch. He was crushed and sat there crying. Inside I felt bad for him but outwardly I put on a show that I didn't care.

I didn't want to talk to him anymore so I stopped delivering papers to his house and started placing them in their mailbox. His parents didn't like this one bit, and called Mom and Dad to tell them. From then on I had to walk to the door to deliver their paper. Fortunately for me, a short time later the family moved out of state and I never saw them again.

Over the next couple of months I had several boyfriends, until one day a guy friend of mine pulled me aside. He said that what I was doing wasn't good.

"If you keep going like this, guys aren't going to think much of you."

"Thank you for letting me know," I replied truthfully. I had never heard this before and I was grateful that he had taken the time to explain it to me. Eventually, he and I began dating.

I would walk to his house each morning, then we would go to school together. Everything was going fine, then something odd began to happen. If he put his arm on my shoulder or tried to hold my hand I would take a swing at him. I didn't want to hit him—at least not consciously; it was a knee-jerk reaction. What I came to realize was that when he touched me it reminded me of my father grabbing me or one of the many other traumatic experiences I had undergone. My body was responding with an uncontrolled reflex; a fight or flight reaction to a possible threat.

This didn't go over very well with him and since I couldn't explain it he eventually broke up with me.

Still, by all accounts I was enjoying a normal teenage life— the most normal I had ever experienced. I had a best friend Rebeka who lived across the street, and I began dating Ed, a wonderful guy, who lived a few houses down the street.

Ed wasn't as touchy-feely as my last boyfriend; in fact, he was content to just hold my hand, which didn't feel so threatening. Sometimes, when we sat on the sofa together, I would even fall asleep with my head in his lap, though I would twitch and jerk as if startled. Ed told me this bothered him, but what could I do?

Then out of nowhere Ellen arrived one day and said I would be moving yet again.

I was confused, but I didn't have a say in what was happening to me. Everyone else seemed to be making decisions for me or on my behalf. I packed my belongings into the suitcase and once again got in the back seat of the car for my journey to who knows where.

It was hard saying goodbye to everyone. I finally felt like I had a family and now they were taking that away from me. It didn't make any sense. I hadn't done anything wrong. I wasn't in trouble. So why was I being moved? When I asked about taking my bike Ellen told me I had to leave it behind.

"You won't be able to use that where you're going."

But where was I going? What does this all mean? All these questions were running through my head but I couldn't seem to ask any questions to get answers. My mind froze and my mouth was silent.

Yet again came the infamous car ride. I sat in silence for a long time until I finally got up enough nerve to ask where she was taking me.

Finally Ellen revealed that the diagnostic center I was in had suggested I would benefit from being placed in a group home type setting. Apparently I had been put on a waiting list and there was finally an opening in such a place.

I was stunned. First of all, I had no idea the place I had thought of as the "juvenile prison" was actually a "diagnostic center." I wasn't even sure what that meant. What I was sure of was that they had made a mistake and there was no way I belonged in a group home, whatever that might be.

At this point the only thing I could do was trust in God. It was good to feel His presence again in my life.

Trust in the Lord with all your heart and do not lean on your own understanding; in all your ways acknowledge Him, and He will make your paths straight. ~ Proverbs 3:5-6 NAS

Naive to Informed

It took several hours to get to St. Mary's group home. When we finally arrived I was surprised to see a long driveway leading to a huge stone building. I wasn't sure what to make of it, but I remember thinking, *If this is a group home, where are all the children?* It was a lot to take in. The place seemed deserted. *Maybe there's a mistake and we have the wrong location.*

We got my belongings from the car and walked up to the entrance. We knocked on the door, but no one answered. Ellen said, "Maybe we just need to go in."

She opened the door and we walked into a large foyer area where there still seemed to be no one around. We walked down the hallway until we came to several doors and then someone heard us and came out.

We entered the office area and took a seat until my paperwork was retrieved. I sat there in silence as Ellen signed all the official documents that now gave these people the right to care for me and make decisions on my behalf.

Once she left I was escorted to the dormitory area and shown where I would be sleeping. Each dorm had four or five cubicles, and each cubicle had room for four girls; every girl had her own twin bed, closet space, and a cabinet. The cabinet had a shelf on top for displaying personal items. There were also two cubicles near the dorm office, but they had space for only two girls. As I later found out, these were reserved for the girls who had been there the longest and earned more privacy.

For the new girls, who started out in the front of the dorm nearest the lounge and TV area, there was no privacy to speak of, and little peace. There was a row of showers and bathrooms along the outer wall by the cubicles, so you had to contend with the noise from everyone going in and out of them, not to mention the noise coming from the lounge.

After I got settled and put my clothes away, my tour guide showed me how to get to the cafeteria and the game room. She also showed me the outside courtyard, where the girls went to get fresh air and read. At first the courtyard, with its twelve-foot-high fence topped with barbed wire, didn't look very inviting.

No one left the facility to go to school; there were classrooms on site and everyone had the same teachers. There was also a nurse's office and they occasionally brought in a dentist for whoever might need it.

After the classrooms, my guide took me to see the gymnasium. This of course was where gym class was held, and I was told that on nice days we would go outside, where there was a large in-ground swimming pool.

We went back inside and my tour guide took me to a little shop on the first floor. She explained that I could go there to purchase toiletries or personal items, so long as I had the money.

"How am I supposed to get money?" I asked her.

She told me there was a work program, where girls earned money by helping in the kitchen or cleaning up around the facility. "Some of the girls' parents put money in their accounts so they can buy things," she added.

"That's not going to happen for me," I said, "but I'd like to sign up for work."

She explained that this needed to be approved but that she

would get me the paperwork.

By the time I had completed the tour it was time for dinner. My guide escorted me to the cafeteria and said, "You'll be fine now, just follow what everyone else does and I'll meet you in the dorms later."

There was so much to take in, but once again I learned to adapt to my surroundings since I really didn't have much choice. Not having a choice had become a constant in my life. I soon learned that life in a group home is basically a repeat of the same day over and over. Every morning started with a shower, which went according to a strict schedule—everyone needed to be in and out of the shower by a certain time. The dorm monitors then led us down to the cafeteria for breakfast; this was followed by a trip out to the courtyard for a cigarette break, then we went off to school. After lunch break, we could go to the game room or back out to the courtyard for another cigarette, then once school was over we were escorted back to the dorms to do homework or hang out in the lounge until dinner. Once dinner was over we could head to the game room or courtyard for another cigarette and games.

I soon got to know all the girls there, and was grateful to have been placed in the dorm I was in. Some of the girls from the other dorm didn't seem very nice.

The ping pong tables were always a big hit, along with backgammon. The dorm monitors were always there to supervise but they would join in playing games sometimes. Then it was back to the dorms for quiet time and everyone had to be on their own beds before lights out. The next day we would get up and do it all over again.

Saturdays and Sundays were different, of course, because there was no school.

The dorm monitors would arrange outings to go skating or shopping, on a picnic, or some other activity. Only a certain number of girls could go and you had to earn that privilege. Everyone would pile in the van, sometimes two, and we would get a lecture about proper etiquette in a public place. If we broke any of the rules everyone would immediately have to return to the dorms.

As time went on, one of the dorm leaders noticed that I seemed a bit naive compared to the other girls. She watched out for me and gave me special privileges. Once I got permission to work, she let me assist Tess, the cook, which was considered a good job.

On Sundays, they arranged for a local pastor to pick me up and take me to church. This was available to any of the residents, but it turned out I was the only one who wanted to go. They also allowed me to go on outings with church people after the service, and this sort privilege was not given to anyone but me.

Tess also took a liking to me, and I found her to be very nice and easy to work for. Sometimes she brought her son to work with her, and after completing my duties I was allowed to go outside with him. We found a path that led up to a fire pit and we would go climb on the stone wall. He seemed to like me as well, and even let me borrow his football outfit for the Halloween party. I enjoyed our time together, but once I learned that he used drugs, I became uncomfortable and avoided hanging out with him.

When I heard they were offering a Karate class, I signed up and found I liked it, especially when the instructor took us outside. On one of those days, as the class ended he gathered everyone together and announced he had lost his pen. It meant a lot to him, he explained, and asked us to look around for it.

After an unsuccessful search everyone returned to the dorm. The instructor had an appointment elsewhere and was about to leave when I asked if I could stay out and keep looking for a while.

He said it would be okay as long as I promised not to take off or break any rules. This in itself was huge because no one was supposed to be unsupervised. It made me feel as though they actually trusted me. I promised him I would just look for the pen until it was time for dinner.

We'd held class in a big field, so I decided to start at one corner and methodically make my way across. Anyone watching me would have thought I looked a bit crazy, walking back and forth with my eyes to the ground, but I didn't care.

After nearly an hour, the pen was nowhere to be found and I was running out of field. Yet all I could think of was what the instructor had said: "This pen means a lot to me."

Suddenly I began to pray. "Please, God, please allow me to find his pen, I don't want him to be upset about losing it."

Sure enough, God came through. Shortly after saying that simple prayer I saw the pen lying on the ground. I was so excited that I would be able to give him his pen back. When I got to his office he had already left for his appointment, so I decided to give it to one of the dorm monitors. I asked her if she would give it to him the next time she saw him.

She assured me she would, and I left for dinner.

The next time I saw the Karate instructor he said, "I'd like to talk to you after class."

After class I went to his office.

He waved me inside and said, "It means a lot to me that you took the time to find my pen. Everyone else gave up but you stuck it out."

"I just wanted to help," I replied truthfully.

"Well, I really appreciate it."

He then handed me a card. "This is for you."

I thanked him and left with a smile on my face. It doesn't take much to make a person feel good inside, and though the card, with his handwritten thank-you note inside, was lovely, all I had really needed was the expression of gratitude on his face.

As the days turned into weeks and weeks turned into months, I continued to make the best of my time in this place. It was often a struggle, especially when parents came to visit their children. I knew I would never have anyone visit me. One visiting day, another girl's father invited me to join them since I didn't have anyone to talk to. *How nice is this?* I thought as I sat there beside them. Imagine my shock when he started talking about *his drugs!* I realized that he was actually supplying his daughter with them.

He then turned to me and asked, "Would you like me to bring you some the next time?"

"No, that's okay," I replied, as if I thought this was normal.

When we returned to the dorms, the girl called me to her cubicle. She showed me what her father had given her.

"You're going to get into trouble if they find that."

She didn't seem concerned. "They aren't going to find it."

One of the things her father had given her was a brown bottle. She brought it up to her nose and took a sniff.

"Here, try it," she said.

I was very hesitant, but I didn't want to look like I had no idea what to do, so I grabbed the bottle and inhaled deeply.

"Take it easy," she said, "or we will get caught."

I felt lightheaded. *What do they see in this? It's not a good feeling.*

On the next visitation day, I was shocked when Stella Petrova arrived at the facility. Unsure how to react, I asked, "How did you know where I was?"

"Ellen told me," she replied, adding that it had been a long drive so she might not make it back again. We had a cordial visit. Stella seemed uncomfortable but stayed until visiting hours were over. In the end I still wasn't sure why she had come, and it would be the last time I heard from her. In the nine months I was in the group home, I would have only one other visitor, this one much more shocking than Stella.

By that time I had been going to church on a regular basis, and sometimes the Pastor would get permission for me to attend outings after the service. Sometimes, it was a visit to people's homes, other times it was lunch with a group of people at the church. There were two college guys, Don and Frank, who attended these luncheons, and though I was really attracted to Frank he never seemed to notice me.

One Sunday afternoon they quite unexpectedly both showed up at the group home. The dorm monitor gave them special permission to visit me in the lounge area. This was totally unprecedented, as no man was ever allowed in the dorm area, let alone to visit a girl unsupervised. I couldn't imagine what they'd said to get the dorm monitor to agree to that.

As we took our seats, Don and Frank on one sofa and I on the other, I made small talk, all the while wondering what this visit was all about. Then the conversation turned to the future and what we envisioned for ourselves. Frank sat back and kept quiet, but Don started asking questions like, "Do you plan on getting married some day? Do you want children some day? If you do have children, what would you name them?"

I answered his questions, never in a million years imagining where they were headed.

Suddenly, Don asked, "Would you consider marrying me?"

Completely stunned, I said the first thing that came to mind: "I'm younger than you." Even as I said this, I was thinking that if Frank was asking I probably would have said yes!

"I'm not really ready to get married," I told him, "I'd like to finish school first."

"I understand that," Don said, "I'm still in school too, but once I graduate from college we could get married if you'd like."

He paused, then added, "I'd like to help you get out of this place and make a nice home for you."

Somehow, I found enough nerve to say, "Thank you, but I really am not ready."

After that there wasn't much else to say. They thanked me for my time and left. They were barely out the door when the dorm monitor appeared.

"What did they want?"

"Don asked me to marry him."

"What did you say?"

When I told her I'd said no, she said, "Good for you," then told me to head down for dinner.

Don's offer to take me out of my situation brought up questions that had been plaguing me since I arrived. Most of the girls at St. Mary's had either been caught doing drugs or had committed some sort of crime. One of them had shot at a cop, while others were considered runaways who couldn't handle their family situation. All I kept thinking is, *What were the people at that diagnostic center thinking? What made them think I belonged in a group home?* I hadn't gotten into trouble. My only "crime" was having parents who didn't want me.

I began to think, *Why do I need to stay here? Girls ran away all the time from St. Mary's. If they could do it, I'm sure I can do it too.* One night I began planning my escape. I had met a lovely family from church; I figured I'd run away and call them. I was sure they'd allow me to live with them.

After dinner the dorm monitors would go out to the courtyard to smoke, and I knew they often forgot to lock the gate or close the doors properly. I started observing their every move to see when I could get out. Finally, the day arrived. The doors were unlocked and the gate was open. As everyone headed upstairs to the dorm after dinner, I decided it was now or never. I went to the bathroom in the lounge, then snuck out through the courtyard and ran as fast as I could.

That's when I realized I had a slight problem. I had no idea where I was or where the family lived. Still I kept going, running through the weeds to stay as hidden as possible. Once I got to the road I stood there for a few seconds and looked back and forth, then decided I had a better chance heading right.

It became dark rather quickly and I decided I needed to make contact with the family. I found a restaurant with a payphone. One day at church they had given me their number and said, "If you ever need anything feel free to call us." Since I had no money, I dialed the operator and had her place a collect call. When they answered the phone, I explained what I had done. They asked me where I was, and when I gave them the name of restaurant they said they'd be right there.

I sat there, thrilled that they'd agreed to come and get me. However, that hopeful feeling was all too brief. As we sat in the restaurant and talked, I quickly realized they did not want me to live with them. They were there to convince me to go back. Finally, I agreed, since I had no place else to go.

Upon returning to the group home I found out they had alerted them after my phone call. St. Mary's staff had asked them to go to the restaurant and try to persuade me to go back. If that hadn't worked they were to call the group home and let staff know where I was. After that, I noticed that they kept a closer eye on me, and I was no longer allowed to go on weekend trips with the rest of the girls.

Though my first attempt at running away didn't go as planned, after a while I decided to try again. Though living conditions at the home weren't terrible, I was sick of being stuck in such close quarters with so many other girls, some of whom were pretty rough. Mostly, though, I just wanted to be on my own. When I heard that Sylvia, a girl I had become close with, was planning to run away to Colorado, I said I wanted to go with her. Sylvia agreed, only to up and leave without me. I soon had another chance, though; her sister Andrea was at a facility about thirty minutes away and attended school at St. Mary's. She too had decided to head to Colorado.

The plan was for me to sneak away to her facility. I was to knock on the door and ask for a certain worker, who would leave the door ajar so she could escape.

It was the middle of winter and bitterly cold the day I left. With no other transportation available, I stood shivering at the side of the road until a man picked me up. When he asked me where I was going, I gave him the name of the local department store in the town where Andrea's facility was located. From there, she had given me landmarks to follow. As we entered the town, he asked me which store; apparently, there were two of them in the area. I didn't know, so he just dropped me off at the nearest one and I roamed around for an hour, wondering whether I was even in the right place. By then it was too dark to find the landmarks. Not knowing what else to do, I finally asked another man if he knew where the place was.

He said he did. I told him our plan and he said he would help me get there. He invited me into his house; he just had to get something from his car and then he would take me.

I thought this was odd, but I took a seat and waited for him. At least I was warm. Time ticked by and he didn't come back; I was getting nervous but figured it was safest to stay put. About an hour later he returned, but he wasn't alone. Imagine how surprised I was when I saw one of St. Mary's dorm monitors standing next to him!

The next day, my friend showed up for school, furious. "How could you tell someone our entire plan?"

"What are you talking about?"

Apparently the guy I'd met the night before lived next to one of the workers from the facility she was in. The guy told the worker our entire plan.

All of a sudden everything made sense. I apologized but she was so upset with me she said she was leaving on her own and not taking me with her. There wasn't anything I could say or do to change her mind.

About a month later, I learned that two other girls, Lori and Lisa, were making a plan to run. This time it was going to be during the day. Everyone knew when and where to meet but by now the dorm monitors had learned to keep the gates locked. We knew we could get to the courtyard but we were going to have to climb over the barbed wire fence. From there we were to head to the town where Lori was from, meet up with a friend of hers, and hop a bus to Colorado. For some reason Colorado was the place to go.

I had never climbed anything that high before, but of the three of us I was the smallest and figured if they could do it, so could I. Sure enough, we all made it over the fence, one, two, three. I was actually quite pleased with myself. I was thinking this time it was going to work out.

Once we reached the end of the property, Lisa suddenly announced that she was going back.

Lori and I looked at her in surprise. "Why?"

"I just wanted to prove to myself that I could get out," she said, "I don't really want to go to Colorado. It's okay, though, I won't tell anyone anything."

She then returned to St Mary's and we left.

From there, it all went very smoothly. Lori seemed to know exactly what she was doing. We met up with her friend, and then we went to a local craft store.

"Why are we stopping here?" I asked.

"We need money for the bus and this is where we're going to get it."

Now I was even more confused. "How are we going to do that?"

"You see that office there?"

I nodded.

Lori's friend said, "The employees leave their purses in there. Just pretend you are shopping and when we say go, leave the store."

I did as I was instructed while they slipped into the office. A few minutes later we left the store and continued walking downtown. The girls searched through the purse, found some money and credit cards and then threw the purse in the bush. I got an uncomfortable feeling in the pit of my stomach. This wasn't right. The feeling increased when I noticed a Dunkin Donuts across the street with a couple of police officers sitting inside. I looked back at the girls and said, "I don't think I want to go any further."

They said, "Why not?"

"I just want to go back." I told them about the police and said I'd just go to them. I was sure they would get me back to St. Mary's.

"Okay," they said, "but wait till we get far enough down the street until you go over there, and don't say anything about what we did."

I promised them I wouldn't say a word.

I waited a few minutes, then approached the cops and explained my situation. They were very nice. They took me to the station and gave me some food. They even offered me a shower—I was pretty muddy because we had run through some creeks to get to Lori's hometown and yet stay out of sight. The precinct had a huge shower room where I got cleaned up, then put on some clean clothes the officers had found for me.

When I was done, they informed me they would need my picture and fingerprints in case I ever got into trouble again.

They took my picture and hung it on the wall at their precinct. Then came the fingerprinting. What a mess with all the ink. Afterward, the officers hung out with me until someone from St. Mary's arrived to take me back. When I got there, I was promptly informed that I would not be helping Tess in the kitchen anymore. I had lost my work privileges.

A short time after that, a woman arrived at the group home. She spoke with the lead dorm monitor, then they asked me if

I would talk to them in private.

"Sure," I said, though I had no idea what this was about. After closing the door to the private room, the woman asked, "When you ran away with Lori, did you stop at a craft store?"

My heart sank, but I said, "Yes."

"Can you please tell me what you did while you were there?"

"I pretended to shop."

She then wanted to know why I was pretending. I became very nervous. I didn't want to say anything because I had made a promise to the girls. She saw that I was nervous and asked, "Were you with anyone else?"

I said, "Yes."

"Here's what we know," she replied. She then told me about the employee filing charges against me for stealing her purse and using her credit cards.

I got upset. "I didn't steal the purse or use any credit cards!"

She informed me they had talked to the other girls involved and they were saying I was the one that did it.

"No way!" I exclaimed, then told her that I had known they were going to take the purse but had left them without touching anything. I even told her where they had thrown the purse, and that I went directly to the police officers after that.

She thanked me for my time and said if she needed anything else she would be in touch. For a few weeks I heard nothing, then the dorm monitor told me that they had found the purse exactly where I said it was thrown. I figured they followed up with the police to verify that part of the story; or, maybe the woman knew more than she was telling me and was just trying to get more details.

As time went by, I had been able to move closer and closer

to that two-person cubicle. It wouldn't be long now before I got some privacy. Then one day I was pulled aside by the lead dorm monitor. She said, "We have a problem here. There's money missing from my office and you were the last person seen in or around the office area."

Immediately my mind went back to the diagnostic center, when I was accused of stealing and stripped searched. *No way, I thought, this can't be happening again.*

I tried to assure her that I had nothing to do with it.

"Do you have any idea who could have taken it?"

I told her I didn't, but as I said the words, I suddenly got a vision. There was a girl, Camila, who lived in the other dorm. The money was in a drop ceiling above her bed.

"I think I might know where it is..." I said, tentatively, unsure how to proceed. Obviously I couldn't tell her I had a vision. I decided to just tell her where I thought it was and leave it at that.

"Camila and Eve share a cubicle in the other dorm. I think you'll find the money in the drop ceiling above Camila's bed."

"Thank you," she said, "I'll check it out and see what we find."

The next day during school, the dorm monitors worked together to check the drop ceiling and to their surprise indeed found something hidden there.

It was not money, however, but two airline tickets. The girls, who were arrested and removed from the group home, had apparently stolen the money, passed it off to someone else—possibly a visitor who then purchased the tickets and delivered them on the next visit. It was quite an elaborate, well thought-out plan that might have worked...if not for my vision! During this time I was still attending church; it was basically my only contact with people from the outside world. There was another family who seemed to take a liking to me, and on Sunday after church invited me to their home. We enjoyed a nice lunch together, and before I knew it the time had come for me to return to the group home. I was about to go when they presented me with a gift.

Inside the package was a plaque with a picture of a hand. A child was leaning on it and there was a scripture verse that read, Isaiah 49:15-16: "Can a mother forget the baby at her breast...Though she may forget, I will not forget you! See I have engraved you on the palms of my hands."

This was a pivotal moment for me, one in which I felt cared about and loved, not just by the family, but God. It was like He had made a covenant with me, and I was going to be okay.

For many years, that plaque would serve as a reminder that even in the toughest times God never left my side. It got lost in a move just a few years ago, but the scripture will live in my heart with me forever.

In a place like the group home, it's easy to feel like time is slipping away from you. One day blends into the next, yet there is also the sense that life is never truly moving forward. One way we marked the time was moving to the coveted cubicles that housed only two girls. As the months passed, it looked like I was soon going to be moved into one of those cubicles. I had worked hard to get here and was pretty excited about it. I still didn't know why I was there, but as long as I was I wanted to be in a more private room. It turned out, God had other plans for me.

One day, out of the blue, the lead dorm monitor took me to her office and said, "I've got a surprise for you."

From her demeanor I could see it was a good surprise, and thought perhaps she was going to tell me I was indeed

moving cubicles. So I was floored when she said,
"How would you like to go back to your old foster home?"
Completely baffled, I wondered for a moment if she meant
Stella, who had visited me shortly after my arrival. But it
wasn't. It was the Greenes.

"Really, but they haven't visited me or anything. Are you
sure they want me back?"

She nodded, then said, "I've been watching you for nine
months. You are different from these other girls." Then she
said the words I had been longing to hear: "You don't belong
here. I've been working real hard to work out the details, and
I've finally got it approved. You are free to go back to the
foster home if you'd like."

I thanked her and said, "I appreciate it so much. I'd love to
go back."

"Well then you'd better go pack your bags, because we
purchased a bus ticket. You're going home."

Becoming Accepted

As the bus pulled into the station in my hometown I could see the Greenes standing there waiting for me. After a brief, but warm welcome back, we got in the car and headed home. Though I had been gone nearly a year, life seemed to pick up right where it left off. I went to my friend Rebeka's house across the street and we had fun catching up on everything that had happened since we had last seen each other. The sad part came when I tried to contact Ed, the boy I had been seeing when I was whisked off to St. Mary's. During my stay there I had written him a letter saying I didn't think it was right to continue our relationship while I was so far away. To be honest, being in the group home made me feel unworthy of having him for a boyfriend, and I certainly never thought I would return.

Now it seemed too late to pick up where we had left off. Though Ed wasn't dating anyone specific he told me he had promised to take a girl to the prom, and he wasn't sure if he and I would be able to get back together again. Clearly, he had moved on.

Though I was disappointed about Ed, I focused on re-acclimating to normal life. I did what most teenage girls did. I hung out with my friends, went roller skating and rode my bike everywhere. The bike really did represent freedom for me. I would ride for miles into neighboring towns and as long as I was home for dinner they didn't seem to mind.

Then one night at dinner Mom and Dad made the announcement that they were taking the family on vacation. I was excited. I couldn't remember ever being on a vacation. Then, just as quickly as the excitement came, the bomb dropped. Mom said that while they were gone Albert was going to be staying with friends of theirs and I would be placed in another foster home.

Talk about feeling rejected! All this time I'd believed they thought of me as part of the family, but if that was the case then why weren't they taking me with them on vacation? Then there was the fact that I had to go to another foster home. Why wasn't I going to stay with family friends as Albert was? Why, why, why? Though I kept my composure, the questions continued to swirl through my mind all evening; in fact, it was all I could think about until it was time to leave for the other foster home. I was sick and tired of never having control over my circumstances and furious with Mom, Dad, and the entire foster care system.

What I didn't yet realize was how in the toughest times, God is intervening on our behalf. In this case I would say that's exactly what happened.

... God meant it for good in order to bring about this present result, to preserve many people alive. ~ Genesis 50:20 NAS

Three years ago I was going through another phase in the healing process and wanted to find certain people who I had lost contact with that had made an impact on my life.

Via Facebook I was able to locate Gretchen, who told me that they had all moved out of state. She and Seth lived far away with their respective families, but she put me in contact with Joyce and Zach. Imagine how amazed I was to learn I was going to a three-day conference close to the town where they lived! I arranged to stay an extra day after it was over so we could visit and get reacquainted.

It was great getting to see them, though I was saddened to hear that Dad had passed away the year before. Zach's wife had also passed, and he was now raising their five children on his own but with the support of Joyce, who lived nearby.

We spent the day at the beach. As the children splashed and played in the ocean, Mom, Zach, and I sat on the beach talking. They seemed surprised at how my life had turned out and were very happy to see that I was doing well.

All I can say is thank you, God, for Your blessings and keeping my paths straight.

As Ellen drove up to the interim foster family's home, I saw a group of people loading stuff into a big old gold Jeep that held a bunch of other people. I had never seen a vehicle quite like it before. There seemed to be kids everywhere.

Ellen pulled to a stop and we walked over and went through the usual introductions, this time to Pap and Mike Sotori. Though I cannot be sure what their initial impression of me was, I imagine I looked like a girl with a chip on her shoulder, who didn't really care about what was going on. I don't remember entering the house itself, just standing outside with my bag on the ground next to me as Ellen slid back into her car.

As we watched her drive away, Pap, said, "You can put your bag in the Jeep, we are going on vacation."

I just stood there in shock. I wanted to say to him, "What?! I just got here, you have no idea who I am, and you're willing to take me on vacation with you?!"

Talk about the flood of emotions ripping through my mind. At this point I must have said something, or maybe he just noticed my shocked expression, because Pap said, "The Sotori family is heading to New York on vacation, and right now you are part of the Sotori family." He smiled. "So, go ahead put your bags in the Jeep and hop in."

I did as he said and joined the others in the big old gold Jeep. Pap and Mike sat in the front seat with the two smallest children, Frankie and Annie. I sat in the seat behind Pap, along with two boys, Gerry and Ron. As the doors closed and the engine was started another amazing thing happened.

"Let's pray for a safe trip," Pap said, and he did. Right then and there he began praying for safety and fun to be had by everyone.

At that moment I thought, "Now this is a real family, and this is the family I want to live with."

I don't really remember the trip itself, except that it was very long. What I do recall is walking around the streets of New York with this very unique-looking family. Frankie and Annie were Native American; Ron was tall and very skinny with blond hair and Gerry was olive-complexioned with dark hair, and I wondered if others could tell they weren't part of the same nuclear family, but the product of five different families united as one. As we stared up in awe at all the tall buildings, I was a bit overwhelmed by the unfamiliarity of this place and the sheer number of people from every conceivable culture and walk of life. Then Pap started telling stories of all the famous people who lived in this town, and who we might bump into if we entered some of the restaurants. He was so matter-of-fact you couldn't help but believe every word he said. The funny thing was, I didn't know any of the people he was talking about, but it didn't matter. He drew you in with every word he said.

At one point we were walking down the street when, right there, in the middle of the sidewalk, was a sandwich board for a Picasso exhibit.

"Look!" I said excitedly. I had always enjoyed art. It was another way of keeping my mind on things that were happy instead of focusing on what was actually happening in my life. Mike walked over with me to see what it was about. She was so sweet, like a mother hen with all her chicks following her every move. She took me under her wing as we read the sign together. Although we didn't actually go into the exhibit, it didn't matter; it was just so comforting to have someone interested in something that I cared about. Then the Sotori's, whom I'd met just hours earlier, bought me a yellow T-shirt with *Picasso* written across the front. To some this may seem trivial, but I was incredibly moved. People didn't just buy things for someone they'd just met. It made no sense at all to me.

Now, when I look back on that day I can't help but think I looked like a troubled teen who needed an extra touch of LOVE. I must have, because that's exactly what I got.

That t-shirt was my prized possession for a very long time. I even kept it after I outgrew it, just so I had something to remember that day.

When it was time to eat, Pap and Mike decided to have an authentic New York experience. We got some food at McDonald's, then sat down on the sidewalks to eat outside! We probably looked like a bunch of homeless people, but we didn't care. It was GREAT!

It may sound like another cliché, but it is true: the greatest things in life have little to do with material possessions and everything to do with having people who really care and are willing to be themselves, no matter where they are.

I don't remember much else about the trip or the ride back to their home. I do remember thinking that my time spent with the Sotori's was far too short and that I didn't want it to end. Upon returning to the Greenes after the vacation, an uneasy feeling had settled in the house, not because they hadn't taken me and Albert with them, but because while we were all gone someone had burglarized their home. The Greenes must have been surprised when they learned Albert had been the one to break in. He was promptly removed from the home, though I don't know what happened to him after that.

I remember thinking, *See if you would have left* me *with your friends, this wouldn't have happened.* But never did I speak those words.

One night a few weeks later, I was getting ready to head to bed when I ran into Dad in the hallway.

"I love you," he said, and gave me a hug.

I was both surprised and unnerved by this. Although to most kids it would be a perfectly normal way to say goodnight, to me it just felt…*wrong.* Looking back, I think my discomfort was rooted not in an inappropriate behavior on his part, but in the fact that my own father had never hugged me or said he loved me. Nevertheless, I told Ellen I wasn't comfortable being around him anymore and asked if it would be possible to be moved back to the Sotori's home.

She agreed to check out that possibility, and within a couple of days I was removed from the Greene's home. As I entered the Sotori's home, I was once again welcomed with open arms.

Many years later, Mike would tell me that on the day
I returned to their house we sat together at the kitchen

table, I said to her, "I smoke. Do you have a problem with that?" I honestly do not remember having that conversation, but I had to admit I could easily imagine myself saying it.

As Mike took me on a tour of the house I realized this was a completely new experience for me. It was the first time I had initiated the move from one home to another, and it was the first time I had chosen the family.

Even the house itself was a dream come true. As I followed Mike upstairs and into my bedroom, I couldn't believe my eyes. There were three large windows and a little alcove for sitting or looking out the windows. There was a desk in that space as well, two beds, a dresser, and a large closet. Even with all that stuff, most of the space remained free and uncluttered. It was the biggest bedroom I had ever seen, so big it didn't even matter that I was sharing with Annie. I remember thinking I'd always wanted to live in a Victorian house and now I was.

There were three other bedrooms on that floor, along with a bathroom and Pap's library. Downstairs there was a large kitchen, a sitting room and a dining room. Beyond that there was a room that seemed set apart from the rest; I'm not sure what it was used for, except maybe Mike's crafts and artwork. What I found really interesting about the house was the staircase that was never supposed to be used. It was like a secret passage or something.

I adjusted to life with Mike and Pap very quickly and with great ease. I never felt unloved or unwanted. I had actually become accepted for who I was: a teenage girl with an attitude.

Pap worked at a local college, which meant we could use the gym. They had a sauna too, and on occasion Mike would take me with her. For the life of me, I could never understand why she enjoyed it. Within minutes, I would find it difficult to breathe, and all I could think was, *When can we get out of here?* I didn't say anything, though, because I just wanted to like what she liked. When she was ready, I would follow her like a good little chick and we would get nice long showers before heading into town. There we would go shopping at the little stores. I don't remember ever buying anything but it was nice walking next to her while she pushed Frankie and Annie in the stroller.

The Sotori's had a deep faith that strengthened and nurtured my own. On Sundays the whole family went to church, and during the week Pap would gather the family around the dining room table and do devotions. I remember one time he asked me to sing. I told him I only knew one hymn. He said, "Whatever it is, we'll sing it."

I'll never forget the look on his face when I started singing "Just As I Am." For some reason I got the feeling that it wasn't his favorite song, but, true to his word he sang it right along with the rest of us.

I also spent a lot of "mother-daughter" time with Mike. She taught me how to French-braid her hair and encouraged me on a regular basis to try new things. Whatever else was going on, they always made time to do things as a family.

As with any family, there were times that things were not so pretty. Times when I got involved with a family down the street that did not have such great morals. They would sit there almost every night, listening to loud music while smoking pot or hash and drinking. I didn't go for the drugs and alcohol—I had tried both there and found it gave me a headache and made my thinking fuzzy. I went because I knew most of the teens that hung out there and I wanted to have friends.

One night I returned from their house to find Pap waiting for me at the door, flashlight in hand.

"Have you been smoking pot?" he asked.

I told him I had not.

He said, "I'm going to check your eyes and if they are dilated you will not be allowed to come in tonight."

For a moment I stood there, my mind racing with fear. I wasn't smoking it, but everyone else was. Would that affect my eyes? Apparently not, because I passed the test and was granted entrance. Still, I decided to limit my visits to the neighbors' which eventually meant those "friends" no longer seemed to have time for me. It didn't matter, though, because I never wanted to worry that I would not be allowed in Mike and Pap's house.

Other than that night, there was nothing overly exciting or dramatic about life with Mike and Pap. And that is precisely why I've included it.

Life shouldn't have all the troubles and turmoil I endured as a child. There was stability in this family. There was security. And although some of the other families had the same thing, but what set Mike and Pap apart was the unconditional love and compassion they showed everyone they gave a home to.

Indeed, they are the only family I have stayed in contact with as an adult. They are the one family my children considered to be their grandparents.

I remember the day my son John asked Pap if he could refer to him as his grandfather. Pap very nonchalantly said, "Only if you call me, Handsome Stud Muffin Pap." Laughter broke out and it was agreed that would be his new title.

A few years ago, Mike and I had our own little "slumber party." For both of us it was a very special time, though Mike was rather shocked by some of the things I shared that night. What I realized was that my life was a secret. My foster parents were never given any information about my past or what I had endured. It was no wonder, then, that no one had known what to do to help me.

Though my time with Mike and Pap was the best I'd ever known, it would, like all my other foster homes, eventually come to an end. Unlike those other places, it had nothing to do with lack of love from them, but from the inner turmoil I had to deal with on a daily basis.

As Mike once told me, "As a teenager you were looking for love from your biological mother. Your mother was simply not able to give you what you were looking for."

Though outwardly I had moved on, thoughts of my real family, in particular my mother, had never left my thoughts. I wondered what she had been doing since I left and if she had any idea where I was. Through random updates I learned that at some point, Josephine and Heidi had been placed in foster care, though both had since returned home. I also found out that Phyllis was no longer living in Mom's house, so why hadn't she tried to get me back? Mike and Pap were wonderful, and though I truly appreciated all they had done for me, I couldn't shake the feeling that I belonged not with them, but with her. I do not remember exactly when that feeling became a nagging voice, telling me to leave, I just know that I started planning my escape.

It seemed simple enough. One night I packed a few things and threw them down the secret passage staircase, thinking I would collect them on my way out. I would then head to the skating rink, where I could hop a bus that would take me to the town where my mother lived. The next day, I wrote a note and placed it on my bed, only to realize I couldn't walk out the front door because there were people in the kitchen. For a moment I debated what to do; I only had a small window of time in order to catch that bus. Finally, I decided to go down that hidden staircase, though I was a little nervous about what I might find. There were no lights back there, and I didn't know why it wasn't used. Were the steps broken and dangerous? With no other choice, I pushed ahead and a few minutes later arrived at the back door. I snuck out, ran down the street and caught the bus in time.

By the time I got to my mom's hometown twenty minutes later, I had started to have second thoughts. I knew what I had at Mike and Pap's, and it was good. What would I find at my mother's? Unsure of what to do and feeling like I couldn't go back to Mike and Pap, I headed to my friend Chad's house and asked to stay overnight. But when the next morning came, I found I was no closer to figuring out what to do.

A few days later, when Chad and I returned home from somewhere, we didn't notice the police car parked out front. We walked inside to find Chad's mother waiting for us, along with some officers. Turns out she had called to report me as a runaway. As they handcuffed me and led me out, they explained that they were taking me to the precinct and calling foster care. Of all the ways I had imagined this playing out, betrayal and arrest at the hands of my friend's mother was certainly not one of them. The worst part was, I was heading back to foster care without ever having made contact with my mom. The question was where were they going to send me now? That question was answered about an hour later when Mike showed up looking disappointed. The officer turned me over to her and we walked out the door, but as soon as my feet hit the sidewalk, I took off running. Why? I didn't really know, except that I still felt it was my mom's responsibility to care for me. Teenagers, particularly wounded ones, don't always understand the bigger picture or what is best for them. They do whatever they feel will ease the pain.

Yet for some reason, I headed not to my mother's, but back to Chad's, where the police had picked me up just hours earlier. Since I obviously couldn't stay there, he arranged for me to go across the street to another friend who lived with his grandmother. She didn't seem to care about me being there, but the next day Chad's mom found out I was across the street and before I knew it the cops were back, cuffs in hand.

I knew they had called foster care again, and I dreaded seeing that disappointed look on Mike's face. Imagine my surprise when Ellen showed up and announced she was taking me to my mother's. For better or worse, my plan had worked.

Back Home

When Ellen told me I was returning home to my mother, I was excited. Though life with her had certainly not been perfect, it just felt right that we should be reunited.

My mother was in the kitchen when we arrived, and though she seemed prepared for our arrival, I knew immediately from the look on her face that this was not going to go as I had planned. After a brief hello and goodbye, Ellen slipped out the door. As soon as she was gone, my mother gestured to the kitchen bar. "Have a seat," she said, as if she was talking to a stranger. My heart sank.

"If you plan to live here," she said as she took a seat on the other side of the bar, "you are going to follow my rules."

"Okay."

"You don't even know what they are yet." "Okay," I repeated. I then sat there, dumbstruck, as she proceeded to go down the long list of things I needed to do or not do in order to stay there. Though I nodded and mmm hmmm'd in all the right places, I was barely listening. I was too shocked by how she was acting. There was no warm welcome, no welcome at all. It was as if she didn't even want me there.

So, this is how it's going to be. When she finally finished her list she said, "Now go get unpacked."

That's exactly what I did, and as I walked through the house the reaction from my sisters was so cold it felt like I was in a freezer chest.

Definitely not what I was expecting.

I tried to shrug it off.

No one came to talk to me or help me get settled in. They just all sat downstairs in the living room until dinner was ready.

Mom had made Kraft Macaroni & Cheese, as usual, adding extra slices of American cheese to give it more flavor, along with fried sliced SPAM and brussel sprouts.

I thought, *Seriously, she knows I hate brussel sprouts,* but I didn't say a word. It was as if the awful dinner was another way of saying she was not pleased to have me back.

Making Friends

I quickly realized my relationship with my sisters had drastically changed, which is to say we didn't have a relationship. I knew Josephine and Heidi had also been in foster care but I had no idea what their experiences had been like or how they managed to get home so much faster than me. Though at this point they were little more than strangers, I was hoping they would be willing to share their stories with me.

It took a while before we even began to rebuild any sort of relationship. Josephine was distant, and definitely different from the girl I remembered. She wore her hair in braids and seemed to think she was Native American, at least that's what she told people. Later, I would learn that the foster home she was in was located in a school district where the people considered themselves to be Indians. Heidi was also distant and it would take a long time for our relationship to become somewhat normal. As for Emily, she would point at me and whisper to her friends, as if she didn't even know me.

In those early days at my mom's I spent much of my time alone. My sisters had their own friends and made it clear I wasn't welcome to join them.

I found myself wandering around town and came across a group of guys playing baseball down at the end of the housing projects. It seemed innocent enough, so one day I took a seat by the fence and watched. Eventually one of them started talking to me, and just like that, I had been welcomed into their group.

Mostly, they played baseball and I watched. Some days we walked around town and at night we would go skating. Then one day, as we were walking through a store, I noticed one of the guys take something. I quickly left the store so I wouldn't get caught with him. Once we were a safe distance away I asked him why he had done that.

"Because I wanted it."

"Did you have money to pay for it?"

"Sure," he replied, "but why pay for it when you can get it free?"

I thought about what he said and decided it made sense. Of course taking things was wrong, but it would certainly be nice to get things I wanted and keep the little money I had. If this guy could do it and get away with it, why not give it a try?

I figured the local pool was a good spot to give it a try. I'm not sure what made me think of it but I knew people tended to leave their stuff out in the open while they were in the water.

I decided to nonchalantly walk by the towels lying on the ground. I could just bend down pick up what I wanted, usually money, and keep walking. No one ever seemed to notice.

By this time I was spending more of my time with the guys, and they quickly saw how good I was at picking things up. They would scope out the area, come and tell me what they wanted and I'd go get it. Then we would walk out and head back to the housing projects.

It was great. They really seemed to like me. I actually had friends.

Soon we graduated from the pool to local stores. The guys would tell me what they wanted and I would go in and get it. When I returned we would celebrate.

One day they asked if I could get them new baseball

gloves. The oldest guy also wanted a stereo for in his car. They started teasing me, saying there was no way I could get all those items.

I was certain I could, and I was determined to prove it. This was going to take a while, though, because I needed to catch a bus to the mall, which was in another town. When I arrived, I headed straight for a store that sold baseball gloves. I had no idea how to determine if a baseball glove was of good quality so I just chose the most expensive ones I could find. I left the store with five gloves in my possession. Next stop, car stereos, and as luck would have it they were right next to the door. Again I looked for the most expensive one, grabbed it, then literally turned around and walked out the door with the box in my hand.

My heart was pounding so hard I thought it was going to come out of my chest. I knew it was wrong but it didn't seem to matter. The guys needed new gloves and I was the one to get them. I was sure we'd be friends forever.

When I returned with bags in hand they stood there in amazement. I shrugged it off, but I was proud of what I had accomplished. We spent the rest of the day celebrating and had a great time.

The next day no one around. I went to a local store and got myself two packs of cigarettes, of course without paying for them. Then I headed to the gift shop in town. I was planning to visit my old friend Rebeka, who now lived in Alabama, and wanted to get her a little something. I found a cute little name plaque for her. Yes, I got it without paying. Then off to the department store I went. I figured I needed a bathing suit so we could go swimming while I was there. I found a nice bathing suit, tucked it in my purse and headed for the door.

As I was walking I heard footsteps behind me, but didn't give it any thought. I could also hear keys clinking. The sound seemed to get faster and louder as I neared the door. As I placed my hand on the door to push it open I felt my arm being grabbed. It was a man I had never seen before. I froze, my mind racing. *Who is this? Why is he grabbing me? What is going on?*

It never occurred to me he was a security guard. First, he was dressed in plainclothes; second, I honestly never thought I would get caught.

"You need to come with me," he said, and then it dawned on me.

"Okay."

He took me to a room in the back of the store and sat me down at a table, then took a seat on the other side. I was still reeling as he began asking me questions.

He wanted to know how old I was, if my parents knew where I was and so on. Then he asked if he could see inside my purse.

Though I was still in shock, I knew I had no choice but to comply.

As he began pulling the items out he asked why there was a bathing suit in my purse.

My response: "I don't know."

That was not a good answer.

Finally, I confessed. I told him I was planning a trip to my friend's and that I needed a bathing suit so we could go swimming.

He then asked if I had taken items from any other stores. I assured him I had not. That was not a good answer either.

Next he pulled out the plaque. "So you were at the gift shop."

It was not a question.

"How do you know that?"

"All stores have tags on their items," he said, "so we can tell where they were purchased."

Well of course they do, I thought, *Why hadn't I thought of that?* Then we got to the cigarettes. Of course I denied taking them.

He asked me where I purchased them.

"The grocery store across the street."

I couldn't catch a break.

"I'll be right back," he said.

I sat there in this little room by myself for quite some time. When he returned he said, "I'm having a hard time believing you paid for these."

I continued to lie.

"Where's the receipt?" he asked.

"In the trash can outside the store," I told him, and was surprised when he went back across the street and dug through the trash. Of course the receipt wasn't there.

Upon his return he informed me that he would be returning all the items to the stores I'd taken them from. Then came the biggest surprise of all.

He asked me my name, which I gave him.

Then he asked, "What's your father's name?"

Immediately I panicked. I didn't want to go back to my dad's. "I don't live with my father."

"That's okay," he said, "I just want to know his name."

I continued to avoid the answer and said, "I live with my mom. Do you want her name?"

He said, "Yes I'll take her name and give her a call, but who is your father?"

Seeing he was not going to let up, I finally told him my father's name.

"I thought so," he replied, "the apple doesn't fall far from the tree."

"What does that mean?"

"I arrested your dad years ago for stealing."

Immediately I was filled with shame. I certainly did not want to be known for anything my father had done, and I vowed to myself right then and there never to do anything like this again.

When the questioning was over I was taken to the police station and fingerprinted. They then took a mug shot and slapped me with a fine for three times the cost of the bathing suit.

There went my trip to visit Rebeka. Everything I had saved went to pay the fine.

I don't know whether the officer ever called my mother, but since I didn't get in trouble when I got home I assume he didn't. Mom recently confirmed this as well; when I asked her if she remembered me being arrested, she said no.

I had learned a few valuable lessons that day, but only one that was truly ironic. When I went back and told my friends from the projects what had happened, they informed me that since I'd been arrested they could no longer hang out with me. Their moms didn't let them hang out with criminals! They never spoke to me again, though they had no problem continuing to play with the baseball gloves I had stolen for them.

As I write this story I can only think of the grace God has bestowed on me and all the others who will accept it.

It brings to mind the lyrics to the song, "Grace Greater than Our Sin":

Marvelous, infinite, matchless grace,
Freely bestowed on all who believe!
You that are longing to see His face,
Will you this moment His grace receive?
(Refrain)
Grace, grace, God's grace,
Grace that is greater than all our sins!

Without God's grace I would have been headed for serious trouble.

Friendless once again, I went home and did my best to close the distance between myself and my sisters.

One day there was a knock at the door. Since everyone else was out, I went to answer it and was shocked to see my stepmother standing there. I stared at her for a moment, then asked her what she wanted.

"I'd like to talk."

"My mom isn't here right now."

"That's okay," she said, "I really came to talk to you."

Me? What could she have to talk to me about? Not sure what to think, I stood there just looking at her.

"Will you come sit in the car and talk to me?"

"Why don't you just come inside?"

"I probably shouldn't," she replied, "I'm not Rosie's favorite person."

You're right about that one.

Though I was still very uneasy, I finally agreed to sit in her car. As I slid into the passenger seat, I kept thinking, what if she drove off? What if she did something to me? No one would even know where I was. I left the door open and kept one foot hanging out.

Molly got into the driver's side and asked me to shut the door so it didn't kill the battery. Oh man, I thought, as I pulled it closed.

But Molly didn't speed away or try to hurt me; instead, she began talking about me and my life, and how, out of all my sisters, I was the only one that would actually make anything out of my life. As she spoke, I couldn't deny the powerful impact her words had on me. Suddenly, it didn't matter what she had done in the past, she was soothing all those places that had hurt me since childhood. As I sat there, soaking in her praise, I had no idea how much those words would continue to influence my choices, in all areas of my life, for years to come. Yet at the same time, I didn't think it was right for me to be the only girl to make something of herself. Even though my sisters and I weren't on the best of terms, I was sure they had potential and deserved a good life, and I wondered why Molly would say otherwise.

Nothing, however, could have prepared me for what Molly said next. She thought it was a good idea for me to come back and live with them! I wouldn't stay in their house, but in a trailer on their property. I would have the freedom to come and go as I wanted, and I could have friends over. I would have my own food and watch whatever I wanted on TV and so on. As she spoke, my uneasiness seemed to fade away, replaced by the very appealing thought of doing as I pleased. And besides, I really didn't have anything keeping me at my mom's. It was pretty obvious I didn't fit in.

It didn't take too much effort for Molly to convince me. Once I agreed to go with her, she said, "Good, now you'll have to write a note to 'Rose'."

The shortened version of my mom's name struck me as odd. In fact, it had a stinging effect, as if I had been bitten by something and could still feel the effects of the venom. I had never heard anyone call my mother that before.

When I told her I didn't have paper or a pen, she replied, "It's okay, I have some right here."

I thought, *Wow, she certainly came prepared.* Little did I know what a huge understatement this was.

"What am I supposed to say?" I asked as I gripped the pen. For the next few minutes Molly dictated and I wrote down everything she said. Once the letter was written she told me to take it inside and leave it on the counter. She also told me to grab my clothes and hop in the car. I did as she said and away we went.

I recently apologized to my mom for writing that letter and told her I didn't mean what was in it. I was so relieved when she said, "It's okay, I knew it wasn't actually from you."

"How did you know that?"

"Your sister left me one that was pretty much word for word."

Apparently, after I left, my stepmother went back and did the same thing with Heidi.

But I didn't find out about that until much later, long after I'd learned the real story behind Molly's invitation. At first, my new living situation wasn't so bad, though the trailer was actually a camper. As promised, she set it up with a TV and food, and indeed I was able to come and go as I pleased. A few months later, though, the weather started getting cold, which meant they had to buy propane to heat the camper. That's when the truth came out.

They bought a couple rounds of propane but I guess it got too expensive because one day Molly came to the camper and told me they now wanted me to move in their home with them.

"Your father didn't really want it, but he finally agreed."

I asked her what she meant.

"When I came to the house that day, it was because your dad didn't want to pay Rose child support." Apparently, my father had received a letter from the courts saying he had to pay so much for child support, but he refused to pay it, which meant he would go to jail.

"Really...." I said, but I really didn't understand.

"Yes, he would rather go to jail then give her a penny," she replied, and though my father wasn't there I could feel his hatred for my mom.

"I don't want him to go to jail again so I came up with this plan and he agreed."

"Oh," I replied but what I was thinking was, *So where does that leave me?"*

"We want you to move into the house," she said as if reading my thoughts. "It costs more than we thought to keep the camper heated."

What a welcoming thought. It wasn't because they wanted me there but because they couldn't afford to heat the camper! Though I didn't want to give up my freedom, I knew I couldn't stay there through the winter, so I reluctantly packed my stuff and headed across the driveway. At least this time I didn't have to go far.

Just a few days later, Molly cornered me. She began by telling me about how my father had inappropriate relationships with his cousin, something she had alluded to years earlier; then, to my horror, she said that while I slept on the sofa, my nightgown rode up and he had seen me uncovered. I stood there, for a moment, completely stunned.

"Sorry," I muttered, not knowing what else to say.

"No problem," Molly replied, "I bought you some pajamas."

Normally it's great to get a gift, but this gift seemed to imply that I had done something wrong. I wore them, because to do otherwise would have been openly defiant of Molly and, in her opinion, inviting unwanted attention from my own father. Every time I put them on I could hear her awful words in my head. As the days passed, Molly would make similar comments about my father or some other disturbing topic. One day, for reasons I will never understand, she decided to tell me about the local drive-in theater—how when the movie was being projected on the screen, you couldn't really hear what they were saying but you could see the movie clearly by sitting outside on the car and watching down over the hill. She went on to tell about how you could watch them making love and all the other stuff they do.

"Okay..." I said, feeling completely creeped out. Why was she telling me this stuff? Did she think I cared about those types of things? Suddenly I found myself wishing I could get out of here. But where? By that time I had burned a lot of bridges, including with my mother.

Yet at the same time, I longed to bond with someone, and since no one else was around I tried to bond with Molly. One day I came home from school and I told her I had a boyfriend.

"What do you think his name is?"

She guessed a few names, all of which were wrong. I stood there rather puzzled, because in my mind I'd figured she would have guessed it right away. When she finally gave up guessing I told her his name was Mark, the same as my dad's.

"What's his last name?" she asked casually.

I told her, then she asked how we'd met and where he was from. This too, I shared with her. I was excited and happy that she was showing an interest in my life, then quickly realized what a mistake that was.

That was a Friday. By the time I walked into school on Monday, I no longer had a boyfriend.

When I asked Mark why he no longer wanted to date me, he asked, "Do you remember your old bus driver?"

For a moment I had no idea who he was talking about. "Who?"

"Do you remember your old bus driver," he repeated, then mentioned the school I had gone to when we lived on the farm.

Immediately my heart sank and my body went numb. "Yes," I said, "but what does he have to do with us?"

"He's now my bus driver and he told us how you used to ride his bus and what you used to do with him on the bus."

I was speechless.

"Look, over there," Mark said, pointing.

I glanced over and sure enough, there he was, sitting in his bus, with a smirk on his face as if he was waiting for me to look in his direction.

Immediately, I knew Molly had had a hand in this. I didn't understand why she would do this, or why the man would tell other students about the inappropriate relationship he had had with me, but apparently he had said something, not only to Mark but to other boys on the bus. He had also convinced them that I had been a willing participant and had possibly traded sex for favors.

I stood there, embarrassed beyond all measure, and angrier than I had ever been in my life, though I didn't know whether I was angrier at Molly or myself. Once again, she had proven just how evil and vindictive she could be. How could I have trusted her?

Even more disturbing was that no aspect of my life was off

limits to her. I couldn't figure out how she knew so many people and what she did to get them to do her bidding.

When I arrived home that afternoon, she asked me how my day had been, something she had never done before.

"It was fine," I replied, refusing to give her the satisfaction of knowing she'd caused me such humiliation and pain. I had learned my lesson once and for all, and I knew I would never confide in her again. The problem was, the damage had already been done, and Mark and I never really spoke again.

I did my best to get through the rest of the school year one day at a time. As much as I wanted to, I refused to run and hide. Clearly, Molly was waging some sort of war against me, and I was not about to hand her a victory.

Fortunately, it was a big school, so there were plenty of other people to meet, people that were not associated with Mark. I started hanging out with Kim, a girl from class. I knew Kim liked to drink, so when I found out we were going on a field trip I came prepared with a thermos of wine. Molly made some at home, and occasionally I would take a sip or two and found it to be pretty good. After filling the thermos that day I filled the bottle back up with water and figured by the time Molly realized what had happened it would be too late to do anything about it.

I was so impressed with myself for thinking of such a brilliant idea, and I knew Kim would be impressed too. As soon as we got on the bus I revealed my secret to her. She didn't believe me at first, so I handed her the thermos and told her to try it. She was definitely impressed, and the next thing I knew she was sharing it with the other kids on the bus. I thought for sure I was a goner, but luckily the chaperones didn't notice. After that we became inseparable.

I eventually made other friends as well, and I also started dating a new guy, Bill. To my relief, Molly seemed to have no connections with his family, and after what had happened after Mark I played things close to the vest as well.

At home, things continued to be tense. One day we were having yet another bizarre conversation and it came to light that my father didn't think he was my father. It wasn't the first time I had heard this, but it was the first time I heard it from him.

Though I was usually a private person, I did share this with some of my new friends. I was shocked when one girl said my dad might be right. When I asked her why she would say that, she told me I resembled a police officer from her town!

"Maybe he's your real father," she added.

I was surprised once again by my father's reaction to the news. He was thrilled, and even wanted to know what the officers' name was and where he was from. When I told him what my friend had said, my dad said he knew the man we were talking about and in fact had known him from when I was born. He agreed it was possible that this man was in fact my biological father.

The conversations didn't end there; instead, my questionable paternity became a daily discussion. While I was overwhelmed by the new development in my already tumultuous life, it was clear from the tenor of these conversations that not only did he not mind if I wasn't his child, he didn't want me living there. Finally, I called Bill and asked if his mom, Janet, would come and get me. She said she would and within a matter of minutes I had packed up my cat and my few belongings. I was all ready to hop in her car, when she said, "You can't bring the cat."

My heart sank once again. My cat was my friend. She was

the one thing in my life that brought me happiness. As I looked at her I realized that for my own sanity I had to let go. I placed her on the ground and she just sat there as if to say, "Why are you leaving me?" I got in the car and we drove away. I couldn't even look back, I knew I had to go, I knew I had to start a new life for myself.

In the exercise of His will He brought us forth by the word of truth, so that we would be a kind of first fruits among His creatures. ~ James 1:18 NAS

Moving On

On the ride to Bill's I filled Janet in on what had been happening at my father's house, specifically, the fact that he and Molly didn't want me there. We then talked about what the next steps I had to take in order to get my life on track. The short-term plan was that I would stay at their home until we could come up with a better living arrangement. At this point I didn't care where I lived, as long as it wasn't with my father and his wife. I was furious with them for misleading and misguiding me and furious with myself for allowing them to do it. Now all I wanted was to get away from them for good.

Though I knew I couldn't live at Bill's home indefinitely, I was a bit surprised when just a few days later Janet approached me with the idea of living with his grandmother. At this point I hadn't even met her yet, but apparently the two had already spoken about me.

When they asked me if I thought I could live with her, a hundred thoughts immediately started racing through my mind: *How far away is she? Will I need to switch schools? What is she like? Will she like me? ...* and so on. Those thoughts became words and I found myself asking the questions out loud.

The answer surprised me. It turned out Bill's grandmother lived only a few blocks away. Filled with relief, I said I thought it would be alright so long as she was willing. And just like that, we were off to meet her.

No matter how many new homes I had walked into, I always felt nervous and unsure of what to say or how to act, and this was no different. It helped that the house was comfortable and well kept. It was also enormous, with a large living room, dining room, kitchen, and bathroom downstairs, and three large bedrooms and another full bath upstairs. The front bedroom was hers and the other she used as a sewing room. I felt like I had just stepped into another world. All this space and she was willing to share it with me.

We had a very nice visit. Bill's grandmother had prepared a meal for everyone to enjoy, and as we sat down to eat the conversation turned to our new arrangement. She said she was willing to let me stay as long as I helped her with the cleaning and her errands. She also thought it would be good if I got myself a job. They seemed like fair requests, and I agreed to all of them. Once again, I had a place to call home.

It didn't take long to move in, as I had so few belongings. Bill's grandmother directed me upstairs and into my new room, which I found to be very comfortable. Indeed, I would feel more relaxed there than I had in a very long time.

When I asked what she would like me to call her, she replied, "My first name, Eunicia." She went into so much detail about the spelling of her name, first telling me the correct spelling then explaining that her sisters had chosen to spell it differently and how she went by their version. Eunicia is actually the Greek version of the name Eunice and means "good victory," so while I always called her by her birth name, I refer to her here the way I thought of her, as "Grandma V."

Grandma V was different from any person I'd ever met. Though not overly demonstrative or expressive with her feelings, I quickly learned I could count on her for a steady, constant, reliable type of love that was always available. In her gentle way, she taught me how to take care of a home. She loved to cook, especially this pickled cucumber salad. It was very simple with just cucumber, onions, and tomatoes and of course the seasoning. She made it all the time. She also cleaned differently than I had ever experienced before. Spring cleaning and fall cleaning meant all the curtains and bedding were removed, washed, and packed away. Thin blankets came out in the spring along with the lace curtains. In the fall the quilts and drapes came out. Dusting meant spraying the rag first and not the furniture. Everything got moved, we didn't just dust around stuff. She enjoyed doing ceramics. We used to sit and paint the different items together, or play Skip-bo or Rummikub. She even got me a job at the same company she worked for, and didn't make a fuss when I decided I didn't like it and found another job elsewhere. As I settled into this kind woman's home, it seemed I was finally putting all the turmoil behind me. Little did I know there was still some unfinished business going on behind the scenes.

One day Grandma V sat me down and explained that we were going to court to finalize some paperwork. My mom and dad would be there as well. I had no idea what she was talking about, and I certainly didn't realize what an impact that day would have on the rest of my life.

We arrived at the courthouse and were led to a special room with a large table in it. Grandma V and I took seats on one side and waited. After a short time my dad and Molly walked in with their lawyer and sat down across from us. It made me uncomfortable, a feeling that grew as I listened to them talk. Although I don't remember everything that was said, I do remember their lawyer explaining to me what was happening, and what the word *emancipation* meant. He explained that from that day on I would be responsible for my own well-being; this included providing for myself financially.

I sat there thinking, *How can this be? Why are they doing*

this? When the lawyer was done talking he asked if I had any questions. Well, of course I did, but there was no way I was going to ask anything in front of my father and Molly.

Instead I just said, "What about my mom?"

"She already signed the papers," the lawyer replied, his tone matter-of-fact as he pointed to where she had signed.

Now I was in total shock. Across from me I had two people willing to sign papers saying they no longer wanted me. In front of me lay a paper signed by my mom stating she no longer wanted me. And now they wanted me to sign the papers saying I was okay with all of this. Hell no, I was definitely *not* okay with this! I was not okay with admitting my parents didn't love me, I was not okay with admitting they didn't want me. I certainly didn't want to admit it in writing! But then again, refusing to sign the paper wouldn't change anything, so I picked up the pen that was presented to me and signed my name. Just like that it was finished. I was no longer their daughter, at least not one they were responsible for.

As soon as I set the pen down my father and Molly stood and, without a word to me, turned to leave. After telling me he'd be right back the lawyer followed them out.

When they reached the door the lawyer turned back again and said, "I'll be right back."

Upon his return he handed me an official document. "This is a copy of the papers for your records."

My records? I didn't have any records, and even if I did I was pretty sure I wouldn't want them to include evidence of my parents' abandonment.

He then thanked me for coming, as if I had a choice and told me to have "a nice day." It might have been comical if it wasn't so sad.

I turned to Grandma V as if to say, *Now what? Are you going to make me leave your home too?*

The ride home was a quiet one. I sat there, brokenhearted, staring at the papers on my lap and wondering what I was supposed to do next. Grandma V sat silently beside me; maybe she felt I needed time to think things through; maybe she didn't know what to say. Maybe she was trying to figure out a way to tell me she didn't want me either.

When we finally got back to her house, I went straight up to my room. She said she was going to make something to eat.

I sat down on the bed and spread the papers out before me. I was still trying to figure out what "Keep for your records" meant. Sure, keep these papers as a reminder of the day my parents signed my life away. Keep these papers as a reminder of the day that made everything I'd always thought over the years true and real. These papers that say, You are not loved; You are not wanted; Go away and don't bother us again.

We. Don't. Want. You.

Grandma V finally called me for dinner. As we ate we talked about what had happened. It was a short conversation because I simply wanted to put it out of my mind and not ever talk about it again.

As the years passed I, like most adults, did accumulate a "keep for your records" file. One day as I was going through it I found these papers. By then I had moved on in my life and forgotten they were there. As I leafed through them, I realized they were merely remnants of an extremely painful past and decided to burn them. It was a deeply healing moment, another step toward freedom.

Recently, I talked to my mother about that day. She

informed me the emancipation was not her decision and in fact she'd been told I had requested it.

So my father and Molly had lied to her. Why did they have to do that? Did they need her signature to make the emancipation official? And why didn't my mom try to find me and ask me? Why, why, why? I added these questions to the seemingly endless list I would never get answers to.

Excuses

That day at the courthouse marked a turning point in my life, in more ways than one. My new status meant working was no longer a choice, but a necessity, and though I tried my best to be a good student, there were days when I was tired. I started skipping school and would spend the day walking the railroad tracks and hanging out on the old bridges that went across the river. They tended to be quiet places with no one else around. There were a lot of railroad tracks to pick from and I could just wander about with no one to bother me.

At first no one seemed to care that I was missing so much school. In fact, they didn't notice at all. I would simply write up a note excusing myself and sign either Grandma V's name or Molly's. It didn't occur to me that one day someone would question why there were two different people signing my notes.

Then one day I arrived home to find Grandma V waiting for me. "How many days of school have you missed?"

Oh no, I thought as I sat down, *the jig is up.*

"I don't know exactly," I replied truthfully. I hadn't kept track.

Apparently, the school had been keeping track, because Grandma V pulled out a piece of paper with a list of dates.

"This is what they sent over." She handed it to me.

"I only know of a few of these days, so what did you do on the rest of them?"

I had to be honest. "I walked around."

To my surprise, there was no punishment, just a simple

conversation about it. How crazy was that? She didn't yell at me, she didn't threaten me, she just wanted me to know that she knew what was going on.

The next day I was called in to see Mr. Collins, the guidance counselor. As I walked into his office, I thought, *Here we go, now comes the punishment.*

Instead, I was in for another surprise. Mr. Collins did not seem angry; he simply asked me to take a seat then informed me that he had spoken to my father and Molly. Immediately, panic set in. Why would he talk to them? What had they told him about me? All lies, no doubt.

He must have seen the horror on my face because he said, "It's okay, I understand what you've been through."

I said, "Really?"

"Yes, they explained how you no longer live with them." He paused. "But I'm confused about why they sign your excuses when you are absent."

Yep, the jig is up, I thought; then, figuring there was no point in lying to him, I admitted I was never sure whose name to sign to the notes when I missed school.

Mr. Collins continued in an understanding manner, even after he found out that many of my absences were not legitimate.

"Do you realize since you are responsible for yourself, you have authority to sign your own excuses? No one has to write one for you."

"No, I did not know that."

He went on to say that considering my situation the school would understand if I needed to take a day off here and there, but I would have to write an excuse every time and sign my own name to it. I thanked him for being so nice and agreed to do my best for the remainder of my school days.

After that life fell into an easy, predictable rhythm. I went to school during the day and to work in the evenings, then it was back home to grab a bite to eat before going to bed. On the weekends I would find time to hang out with Bill and his friends. We would go to parties, go fishing and camping, or just watch a movie. Things had become so normal, it was sometimes hard not to wonder if it was all too good to be true.

A Defining Day

As time went on I began to see a different side of Bill, though later I would realize I had known from the beginning that it existed; I just didn't know how bad it was. Bill liked to drink, a lot. Most of the time it was just beer but when he got hold of the stronger stuff it wasn't pretty.

One night he came home from a party and started beating on his car. It started with swearing and screaming and kicking it, then he grabbed a baseball bat and started smashing it. I just stood there, terrified, and watched the scene unfold. It was a big relief when Janet finally came home. As she took him inside I heard her ask him what he'd had to drink. He replied, "A bottle of gin" and I made a mental note to keep him away from it in the future.

As time went on he drank more and more, and he was drinking the stronger stuff much more regularly. I never quite knew how he got it but when he went out with certain friends I knew he would come back violent. It never occurred to leave him, though, because he loved me.

Bill and I had also begun having more of an intimate relationship. When we were at his house, Janet gave us our space, which meant we had plenty of time to be alone together. We were both still in high school and trying to figure out what our futures were going to look like.

Like most teens, I didn't know what I wanted to do or what I wanted to be. I thought I wanted to be an artist, but to me that meant living in a big city. It was a scary thought.

As for Bill, it seemed he wasn't interested in any plans that didn't include a bottle. I watched him sink deeper and deeper into alcohol and eventually drugs as well. I found myself growing increasingly uncomfortable going to parties and eventually I stopped going altogether.

One day, Janet decided it would be good if I go to the local clinic to inquire about birth control so in case "something happened" between us we could take precautions. I didn't tell her that things had already been happening, I just agreed to go and hear what they had to say.

During the appointment we discussed the different types of birth control available and what I would be most comfortable using. As I sat there, slightly overwhelmed by all if it, I began to realize that despite all my experiences there was a lot I didn't know about life. I also began to realize how far away from God I had gotten. Something about sitting in this office just didn't feel right, yet I stayed. I felt I had to do as my boyfriend's mom asked me to do since she had brought me here.

During the conversation the woman suggested I have an exam so they had something in my file in case I came back. I agreed, never in a million years imagining what would come next. When the exam began, she asked, "Could you be pregnant?" It was a routine question, and certainly under-standable given the fact that I was there asking about birth control, yet it took me completely by surprise.

"What?!" I exclaimed. Though there was a possibility, I hadn't missed a period. Besides, it was simply unthinkable.

She asked me if I'd be willing to take a pregnancy test.

Again I agreed, but now I had begun to feel scared. What did she know that I didn't know? Why was she asking me to do more tests that I hadn't intended on doing? A whirlwind of thoughts and emotions engulfed me. What would I do if I was pregnant? But I can't be pregnant, I reminded myself, because I haven't missed. When she told me the test was positive I felt as though my world was crashing in around me. From that moment on the woman's demeanor towards me seemed to change. Janet was asked to come into the room, and as she sat there looking at me all I could feel was shame. I felt like I had let her down. I felt like I had disappointed her. Even though she hadn't said anything yet, I knew she was upset. She had to be. The woman from the clinic started sharing the information with Janet as if I wasn't even in the room. I no longer existed in that space and time. It was such an odd, uncomfortable feeling and place to be. The woman gave her a list of things to consider and a list of possible options.

Not once did she ever address me or ask me how I felt or what I thought or what I would like to do. Not once! Although it was my body we were talking about, I was still a minor and apparently had no say about what was happening.

Looking back, it is rather ironic that this happened just a short time after I signed papers stating I was responsible for my own actions and decisions. I guess the adults at the clinic had forgotten about that tiny factor. But then again, so had I.

The drive back to Bill's house was silent. I was right, Janet was upset. When we got there Janet sat me and Bill down at the table and explained what she'd been told, as if I hadn't been sitting with her when she found out! Once she was done talking she said, "I have to figure out what I'm going to do." Then she left and went to see Grandma V.

Now all I could think was how upset Grandma V was going to be. *She's not going to let me stay at her house, I'm going to have to find a new place to live, now what am I going to do?*

As it turned out, I wouldn't have to figure out anything, because within days of finding out I was pregnant, I was informed that I would be having an abortion. My heart was troubled in ways that I could not understand.

"How is that going to happen? I have no money to pay for something like that."

The response was, "It's being taken care of."

Again, I had no choice in the matter; I was just expected to do as I was told. I just wanted to run away. I wanted to hide, but I had no place else to go.

Maybe it would have been different if Bill had stood by me, but I felt him growing more and more distant.

A few days later, Bill's mom drove me to a different clinic in a different city. I didn't understand why we did that. I figured I wasn't allowed to ask questions because I wasn't in charge and it wasn't my money paying for what was about to happen to me. Upon arriving at the clinic I was escorted into a private room. Janet said she was going to take care of the paper work and she would see me later.

Now I felt completely alone. I was in a strange place. I had no idea even what town we were in because it was so far away. I had no idea exactly what was going to happen to me. All I knew was that I didn't want to have an abortion and I wanted to keep the baby. That's what I knew, but no one had taken the time to ask me how I felt or what I thought. I knew from the time I had attended church that this was not something that should be happening and yet somehow I didn't have a say in it.

As I sat there waiting for someone all I could think to do is pray. It wasn't an elaborate prayer by any means. I just simply asked God to help me make sense of what was going on and send someone who would listen to me. Just then the door opened and in walked a nice-looking lady who introduced herself as Mary. She sat down in the chair opposite me on the other side of the table.

She began to talk to me and explain what was going to happen today. She explained the procedure and how long it takes. She also explained what to expect afterwards and then she asked me if I had any questions.

I told her I understood what she said but I really didn't want to have an abortion.

Mary looked surprised and said, "Oh, I thought you requested to have this done."

I said, "No, I don't have a choice because my boyfriend's mom is paying for it."

"Wait here a minute," she said, "and I'll be right back."

As she walked out the door, my heart did a little skip of excitement. I thought there may be hope after all. I heard her discussing what I had just said to someone else outside the door. Then there was silence as they both walked away.

Upon her return, her face said it all. There was no hope. She didn't even have to tell me. Sadness set in and again I felt completely alone.

Mary sat down again and said, "We're going to do an exam before we begin the procedure, just to make sure everything is okay." It was said in a matter of fact way that I knew I just needed to do whatever they said.

She asked me to follow her to the exam room. She asked me to change into a hospital type gown and she would be back in a few minutes.

I did as she said. When she returned she instructed me to lie down and scoot forward and said to put my feet in the stirrups. She then proceeded to do the exam. Then during the exam she asked me how far along I was. I said I didn't know for sure because I hadn't missed my cycle.

"I don't think we can do this," she said, suddenly sounding concerned.

"What's wrong?"

"From the size of the baby, you are already in your second trimester and we don't do abortions past the third month." She paused. "I think your wish just came true."

I remember she smiled at me and I smiled back. I said, "Thank you."

"I need to go and let the doctor know what is going on."

As she walked away, I finally felt relief and a tinge of happiness that they couldn't go through with the abortion. Inside my head I was celebrating, *YES, YES! Now I get to keep the baby.*

I could hear her speaking with another individual but I couldn't make out what was being said. Then I heard a third voice. I recognized the voice as Janet's but I still couldn't make out what was being said. The uneasy feelings began to return.

Moments later Mary returned to the room with a look of defeat on her face. Once again I knew just by looking at her that they were still going to do the abortion.

"What happened?" I asked.

"The doctor said it will be okay and he's still going to do the abortion."

Although I knew this woman was trying her hardest to give me support, I also knew she had no say in what was about to happen, just like I had no say in the matter.

"Sit tight, someone will be in to get you as soon as they are ready. Would you like me to stay with you during the procedure?"

"Yes, I would like that," I replied. After all, Mary seemed to be the only person there that cared about my feelings.

Before I knew it I was escorted to yet another room. This one was smaller with just a bed for me to lie on, a chair in the corner for Mary to sit on and at the foot of the bed was the machine the doctor and his nurse were going to be using. It was all formalities at this point. The doctor asked, "Did they explain to you what was going to happen today?"

"Yes."

"Okay then, let's get started."

He proceeded to give me some instructions, but it all went in one ear and out the other, like a blur.

I do remember Mary bending down and asking, "Would you like it if I held your hand?"

"Yes, I would like that."

The procedure took several minutes and at times there seemed to be something going on that the doctor didn't want me to know about because he would whisper things to the nurse and she would whisper back.

As she promised, Mary held my hand the whole time and assured me it was going to be okay.

I just wanted to tell her it wasn't going to be okay because I didn't even want to be doing this. Instead I lay there silently, thinking how I was doing something terrible and God would never forgive me. After all, how could He if I was allowing someone to hurt one of His precious babies? How could this be happening? How could I allow it to happen? I had no answers, only questions and guilt.

Although I had sustained all the physical, sexual, and mental abuse from others throughout my life, as I lie on that bed allowing this to happen to me I realized this was the worst day of my life. There was no way I could change things now.

Now I had to live with this awful day and know I allowed it to happen to me.

Finally, the doctor said, "We're done here."

He then continued by telling me, Mary would help me get to the recovery area and give me instructions.

Mary explained that bleeding was normal and there would probably be blood clots when I went to the bathroom and that that was normal also. She told me that they needed to keep me here for observation for a while until I was able to go to the bathroom and make sure nothing unusual was happening. She told me if there were larger clots they would have to recheck things to make sure everything was okay.

I stayed in the recovery area for what seemed like forever. Other girls were leaving, while other girls had a boyfriend or parent sitting with them. Mary came back to check on me and asked if I wanted Janet to come back.

"Sure," and she told me she would go find her.

When she returned, Mary informed me that Janet hadn't stayed in the building. Apparently the receptionist or someone had told her how long the procedure would take and Janet had decided to go shopping.

I lay there, speechless. Mary looked at me sympathetically and said she was sorry but needed to continue with her work.

Lying there alone I realized I had no one to look out for me except me. There was no one to care about what was going to happen in my life except me. There was no one, no one except me.

I had a decision to make and I decided right then and there that no one, and I mean NO ONE was ever going to make me do something, ever again, that I did not want to do. No one was going to make decisions for me ever again. No one was going to tell me I needed to do anything.

I may not have been an adult yet but I was smart enough to know that what had just happened was not what I wanted. If no one was going to be there to support me, I had no reason to let them make decisions for me ever again. I do believe that was the day I became an adult, maybe not in legal terms but in my mind.

Eventually, Janet returned, just around the time the clinic was closing for the day. They gave me more instructions and said if I needed anything, I should call them on the emergency phone number they provided.

I was glad Janet didn't speak on the ride home; I was too drained to do anything but lay my head against the passenger side window and stare out at the world going by. I tried not to think about what I had just been through but the painful cramping in my abdomen made it impossible. At least it was a Friday, which meant I could crawl into bed and rest for the next couple of days. Those days turned out to be anything but restful, however. The pain was getting worse, not better, and when my stomach began to swell I asked Janet to call the clinic. They told her to bring me back down the next day.

We got there very early in the morning so I would be the first patient in. By then I was literally doubled over in pain, in part because I had not been able to go to the bathroom for the past twenty-four hours and had a completely full bladder. As soon as I walked in they took me back in to the small room where they had performed the abortion.

The thoughts were racing through my head. Was there another baby? Was I going to die? What would happen to me? No one was talking to me; they just started doing whatever they were doing.

The doctor said he was going to have to catheterize me so he could drain my bladder in order to see what was going on.

I had no idea what that meant but by this point I really didn't care. After he was finished with draining my bladder, they did more work with the machine in the corner and then said, "Okay, you should be fine now."

There was no recovery time this time; I was just told to get dressed, then the doctor escorted me to another private room where Janet was waiting.

"She should be fine," he said as if I wasn't in the room, "We drained her bladder and when we did the exam we found..."

I'm not sure what he actually said at that moment, but I did hear him say, "Have her take this medication and make sure she stays out of the sun while taking it."

I immediately took the first dose, then we once again walked out of the clinic. I prayed I would never have to set foot in that dreadful place again.

As we climbed back into the car I asked Janet to please take me to her house instead of directly to Grandma V's. I had not seen Bill in several days and I needed to speak to him. When I got there I gave Bill a hug but he didn't respond in his usual way. Instead I got the cold shoulder. I tried to talk to him but he refused. Finally I decided to go home. Clearly something was bothering him, but I didn't feel up to figuring out what the problem was.

A few days later I went back. I chose a time when I knew Janet wasn't home, thinking Bill might open up if we were alone. He let me in but again seemed distant.

I told him we need to talk but couldn't get him to say anything. Then I asked him if he still loved me. The words that came out of his mouth cut through my heart like a knife.

"I can't love someone who would get rid of my child."

I was crushed. "I thought you were okay with the situation."

"You never even talked to me about how I felt."

Yes, I thought, *because I wasn't given an option.* "My mom said she was taking you to get it done," he added bitterly. For the first time it hit me: Janet had never asked him what he wanted either.

I wondered whether she'd told him it was my idea; if so, she wouldn't be the first person who had lied about me. But it really didn't matter; that was the impression Bill had gotten. Then he dropped the final bomb: he wanted nothing more to do with me. For a moment I just sat there, overwhelmed by a second staggering loss in as many days. I wanted to tell him it wasn't my idea, that Janet had made me do it, but I didn't even have the strength to defend myself. I just wanted to be alone.

I walked back to Grandma V's house and once again went straight to my room. I had nothing to do except be by myself. She was at work and the place was quiet. I threw myself on to the bed and cried. I cried until my body was completely drained of energy. I cried myself into a deep sleep.

Graduation

When I awoke it seemed a week had passed. The entire world felt different, and I, irrevocably changed. As I sat on the edge of the bed it dawned on me that no one else was going to look out for my best interest; I needed to step up and take charge of my life.

That was the moment I realized I was a fighter; a warrior, even. I had gone through some really tough stuff—stuff that would have broken other people—and yet here I was, still fighting to survive in this world. Now I just needed to own my vigor and take steps in the right direction.

But what was the next step? Graduation was only a few weeks away, and then the future stretched out, vast and unwritten, before me. I didn't even have a boyfriend to consider anymore. It was overwhelming, so for now I decided to just focus on finishing school; there would be plenty of time to figure out what came after that.

In the meantime, I decided to celebrate my graduation. It was a significant milestone for any kid, and even more so for one who had achieved it despite considerable odds. I was actually graduating twice that year—from the regular high school and from the affiliated vocational school, where I had been studying Commercial Art. Grandma V felt the same, for when I asked if I could have some people over for a graduation party, she immediately said yes. She even said she would make some food.

I kept it simple, inviting a few close friends and my sister Josephine, with whom I had gradually reconnected with during senior year. I wasn't sure what this party would be like, but it was the first time in forever that I was having my own company, and it felt good.

Josephine, who was also graduating that year, was having her own party at our mother's house. I wasn't invited to that party because Mom didn't want me there. At this point we weren't even on speaking terms.

I told myself this didn't matter, that when she saw me getting my diploma she would want to talk to me again. Since Josephine would be having her graduation party after graduation I chose to have a graduation party from the vocational school. After all with the exception of my oldest sister everyone else that was coming went to that school.

It worked out perfect. I attended graduation at the vocational school and had my party a few days later. Everyone I had invited showed up, and we spent the afternoon talking and eating great food. It was a good day.

Graduation from high school took place the following week. Josephine and I sat side by side, and she pointed out our mother, sister, and grandmother in the crowd. Despite all that had gone on, my heart was happy at finally seeing them again. I figured once the ceremony was over I'd walk over with Josephine and give everyone a hug and say hi.

As I sat there I realized I didn't even care about the actual graduation; I just wanted to see my family again. Finally, the ceremony ended and all the graduates were ushered to the area of the school designated for cap and gown return. Somehow I lost Josephine in the crowd, and I hurried to try and find her. As I was heading out the door I caught sight of her walking with the rest of the family. When she heard me calling out to her she turned back around.

"Let's go talk to Mom and Grandma," I said.

Josephine shook her head. "No, you can't do that."

"Why can't I?"

"They don't want to talk to you."

Somehow I managed to mutter, "Oh, okay, that's fine, tell them I said hi."

She said she would give them the message, then she gave me a hug and turned to leave.

How many times did I need to get my heart broken before I learned? I told myself I couldn't let it get to me, and especially not in public. As I stood there, trying to pull myself together, I spotted Grandma V walking toward me, with Janet in tow. Somehow I managed to put a smile on my face and went to greet them. The three of us went out for dinner to celebrate, and then, just like that graduation was over. It was time to figure out what was next.

Contact with Josephine became sporadic after that. I kept telling myself it was okay, that I had survived much worse losses. Then, just as one sister faded from my life, another stepped back in.

"I want out," Heidi declared, "and I want to know how you did it."

I was at a loss for words, first because I was shocked she had reached out to me after all this time, and second because I didn't know what she was talking about. As we continued to talk it all became clear—she wanted a place to live that wasn't with my mom. I said I didn't know what I could do but I would ask Grandma V what she thought.

It turned out that Grandma V's sister Evelyn was willing to have Heidi live with her. It was like a gift, not only for Heidi, but for me as well.

After that, life fell into an easy rhythm. Most days, I'd come home from a long day at the ribbon factory where I worked, eat and go to bed. Sometimes, I played a card game with Grandma V, sometimes Heidi and Evelyn came over and we all played a game together. Grandma V and I continued this routine for the next two years. Heidi only stayed about six months until she married a man in the Navy and moved away. During this time I also found myself drawn back to God. I became active in the local church and helped with summer Vacation Bible School (VBS) programs and afterschool children's programs called Good News Clubs. I loved doing something to help others; it felt good, like my life finally had a purpose.

I began taking Biblical Study classes and was ecstatic when I finished the first two with As.

One of the guys at church had been a classmate back when I was in foster care. He was part of a Christian singing group, and though I didn't know anyone else they immediately accepted me as one of their own. I soon began traveling with them from concert to concert.

I became particularly close friends with Eric, the sound technician. He was doing his college internship at the nursing home where I worked, and whenever he was there my day was a little brighter. I enjoyed my work and I loved spending time with the residents but it was even nicer having someone my own age to talk to while I was working.

I finally felt happy.

One day Eric became ill and had to be admitted to the hospital. While visiting him that afternoon, I found myself reading the Bible. I read until he asked me to stop, then we talked for hours. Though we had known each other for a while, this was the first time Eric and I shared any personal information. I learned that after college he planned on becoming a pastor. He also told me that his family had some struggles that were bothering him. Listening to him made me realize that I wasn't alone, that everyone was dealing with family stuff.

I was most interested to hear that before attending a four-year university he had first gone to junior college. I had never even heard of such a thing. As we spoke, the conversation turned to the possibility of me attending college. I started thinking about what I would want to study.

Thankfully, Eric recovered, and after his release from the hospital we continued to grow closer. We were not dating; it was just a healthy friendship that felt good. Many of our conversations centered around the future, and I began to give college more serious thought. I talked to Grandma V about it and she said she thought it might be a good idea too.

Deciding I wanted to go to college was the easy part; I still had no idea where I should start or where I should go. Eric suggested I might try the junior college too; it was a great place to figure out what you want to do. He told me the administrators help guide you and you don't need to take the college entrance exams prior to going; they would help me get those done during my first semester. It all sounded like a perfect fit.

He told me it would be a place to find myself and figure out what God wanted me to do with my life. Now the only problem was, how did I get there? Once again, Eric stepped up, this time offering to drive me. I felt it was a terrible imposition—after all, the school was over two hours away—but he insisted, saying he didn't mind if it would help me be who I needed to be.

I really liked this guy and began to think, maybe someday we could be more than just friends. That day would never come, however; Eric did drive me to school and helped me get settled in. We hung out for a short time and then he said he had to go. We hugged, he got in his car and drove back to his college. Although we stayed in touch for a short time, I never saw him after that day.

Here I was in a new town where no one knew me. No one knew about my past, and no one had anything bad to say about me. This was it, a fresh start, a new beginning.

As I unpacked the rest of my belongings and sorted out my books, I decided I was going to make the best of this. I was going to be the best person I could be. I was going to get to know as many people as possible and make real friendships that would last a lifetime.

I loved getting to know everyone. It was a small campus, so everyone was constantly together—in classes or at chapel. We'd go out for pizza at the local pizza shop and then study. I loved being at college and the freedom I felt. I felt freedom from my past and freedom to make my own choices. I had no idea how short-lived that feeling would be.

Remembering how much I'd enjoyed helping others at the nursing home, I chose to focus my studies on social work. It was a challenging program, with a lot of homework and heavy reading assignments, many of which involved history. I had always struggled with that subject, and as the days wore on, I found myself reading and rereading the materials and yet still not understanding it. I found myself getting further and further behind on my reading assignments, which meant more and more time spent alone in my room studying. Over time I found myself feeling more and more trapped, like I was back in that juvenile prison. It didn't help matters that the place was a similar concrete structure.

When I got a poor grade on my first final, I knew I needed help. I went to the counselor's office and told her about my past and how I felt trapped in the building because it reminded me of the juvenile prison. She said she understood but encouraged me not to drop out. She said she would talk to some of the other people who worked there and see what could be done.

In the meantime I had talked to Grandma V and told her how things were going. I told her I might be coming home if she was okay with that. She said that if that's what I needed to do, it would be fine.

A few days later the counselor called me into her office and said there wasn't much that could be done about my living situation at the school. She then made me an incredibly kind offer: I could stay at her home. She was even willing to bring me back and forth to school every day.

Though I was moved, I remember looking at her and thinking, *This will never work. I'm sure something would go wrong, just like it always does.* I didn't say it out loud, of course; I just thanked her and said, "I think I'm going to drop out and go back home."

That same day I received a phone call from Grandma V's son. He was pleasant enough but I couldn't figure out why he would be calling me. That became clear a few minutes later, when he told me he had talked to Grandma V and they decided it wouldn't be good for me to go back to her place because I "caused her too much stress." I felt like I had been stabbed in the heart. *Here we go again. No place to go, no place to call home.*

I realized he was still speaking. "Do you understand what I'm saying?"

"I think so," I replied.

"I don't want you to return to her house."

"Okay," I said, "I understand."

Immediately my mind began to race. Now what? What was I supposed to do? I had just turned down an offer of a place to live, I no longer could go back to Grandma V's and I had already decided I wasn't going to stay in college. Then I remembered Heidi. She and her husband Randy had recently moved to the area. Maybe she wasn't too far away.

I managed to contact her and explained the situation. She said I could come and stay with them until I found something of my own. I now had a plan. This had to work.

To make myself useful, I started babysitting for their one-year-old son Caleb while they were at work. Eventually I was able to find a full-time job at another nursing home, work I was comfortable with and knew how to do. I took the third shift so I'd still be able to watch Caleb during the day. This worked for a few months, but it eventually became apparent that having a third wheel around was taking its toll on Heidi and Randy's relationship. We all agreed it would be better if I found a place of my own.

This place turned out to be a boarding house owned by an elderly woman named Barbara. The rent was reasonable and the room was furnished, so I didn't need to worry about buying anything. It was perfect.

The New Year

While my new living arrangement was affordable and convenient, it was also lonely. Working the third shift was exhausting, so when I wasn't working I was usually sleeping. The upside to working late at night was that most of the residents were sleeping, so we had a lot of downtime. I became friends with Kara, one of my coworkers, and occasionally she invited me over to her house. Her two daughters, Laura and Kayla, were actually closer to my age and we spent a lot of time hanging out.

Shortly before New Year's Eve, the three of us made plans to go roller skating. However, when I arrived at Kara's that night Laura told me they didn't feel like going after all. When she saw how disappointed I was she offered to call their cousin Charlie and see if he would be willing to take me.

"No," I said, "I don't even know him. Why would he want to take a stranger roller skating?"

"He's a nice guy," Laura said, "and he might want to go too."

Finally my desire to go roller skating overcame my discomfort and I told her to go ahead and call him.

When Charlie answered Laura explained who I was and how she and Kayla had backed out of our roller skating plans. She then asked him if he was interested in going, and though I wasn't on the line I could swear I heard his hesitation. Laura went to hand me the phone but I shook my head.

"Here," she said, "He said he'll talk to you."

After a moment I took the phone from her and placed it to

my ear. The conversation was a bit awkward but worth the effort. We exchanged pleasantries and shared a little information about ourselves, and by the time we hung up my evening of roller skating was back on. I decided it didn't matter who I went with, so long as I went.

Charlie came to Kara's to get me. When I first saw him, I remember thinking, he looked a bit dorky but reminded myself that wasn't important. After all, it was just roller skating, not a whirlwind romance.

The conversation was stilted as we headed to the skating rink. It seemed like we were both struggling to find things to talk about. When we got there I hurriedly put on my skates; Charlie on the other hand was moving much more slowly. As soon as the music started I said, "I'll see you out there on the floor," then headed toward the floor without waiting for a response.

"I'll be there in a few minutes," I heard him call out.

I was totally in my element, enjoying the beat to the music while flying around the rink. I was skating forward, backwards and by the time he made it onto the skating rink floor I had gone around several times.

I quickly realized why Charlie was so hesitant to go skating; he really wasn't that good at it. Each time he circled the floor I had gone around a few more times. I realized I needed to at least spend some time with him. After all he had been nice enough to bring me.

When a slow song came on I skated over to him and turned around so we could skate face to face. We still didn't have too much to talk about but he seemed like a decent guy. Before I knew it the evening was over and I reluctantly changed back into my own shoes. As for Charlie, there were certainly no fireworks between us but I exchanged numbers with him anyway. I figured if nothing else I'd made a new friend, a rare commodity for me.

When several days passed and I hadn't heard from him, I found myself picking up the phone to call him. I didn't know too many people in the area and I was itching to do something fun. Charlie said he would like to go out with me again. The second date was not much more comfortable than the first; Charlie reminded me of a stray dog—the kind that look all matted and straggly but eventually begins to grow on you.

That's exactly what happened. We began seeing each other regularly, and I learned more about him and his family. His mom and dad's names were Ruth and Calvin. The three brothers were Cal, Joseph, and Elmer. Everyone lived at home except his older brother Cal, who was already married. They were actually *normal*.

Charlie also seemed too good to be true. He lived on his own and had a full-time job. He knew how to drive and get to places that weren't just in the neighborhood. These things may seem trivial to most people, but to me they were impressive. He took me to nice restaurants and to concerts; he played on a softball team, and I went to his games to cheer him on. But it wasn't just the fun things we did; I also felt I could trust Charlie with anything, though I still hadn't told him much about me, certainly nothing about my painful past. After all, I had trusted people before only to be devastated.

Despite my fears, I eventually realized I was willing to consider a serious, long-term relationship with him. I even started thinking about marriage, something I had never been interested in but found myself discussing with Charlie on a regular basis. He must really care about me, I thought, if he was talking about spending the rest of his life with me.

A few months later I started not feeling well; my stomach

hurt and I was lightheaded. I gave it a few days but when the symptoms didn't subside I made an appointment with a doctor not far from Kara's house. I had been spending more time there lately since she lived near Charlie, so going to a doctor near her house made sense. I walked to the office, only to find that he had ordered some tests done at the hospital. I didn't know what the tests were for, or how I would get there.

I decided to call Charlie's mother, Ruth, who worked at the hospital. When I told her what was happening, she said she would take me. She didn't say anything to me about the tests, though I later found out she knew exactly what they were for. Once the tests were completed, I sat on the bed anxiously waiting for the technician to give me the results. Of all the things I was worried about, it never occurred to me that I might be pregnant.

When I heard the news I was shocked; however, that's where the similarities ended. This time I was an adult—in fact, it was my twenty-first birthday—about to marry the father of my child. And though being intimate before marriage was frowned upon, there was no talk of having an abortion. Ruth did ask me if it was really Charlie's baby, or if I had gotten pregnant before we met and tried to say it was his.

Charlie came to see me as soon as he got off work. I was lying on Kara's sofa, trying to fight off the morning sickness that seemed to last all day. The front door was located directly in front of the sofa and when he entered, I immediately saw the bouquet of red roses in his hand. They were in a sorry state.

He had purchased them in the morning before heading to work and apparently left them in the car all day. By the time he arrived at the house they were all wilted from the heat. It didn't matter to me, though. No one had ever bought me roses before. I was delighted.

He apologized for the roses, then got down on his knee beside the sofa, handed me a little silver box and asked me to marry him. I wish I could say I was filled with joy and happiness. Even though we had been talking about this, I now had a baby growing inside me and I had to make sure I was making the best decision for both of us.

"Thank you so much," I replied, "but I need time to think about it." I then told him I was heading home to see Grandma V and would give him my answer when I returned.

Charlie accepted my answer but had the look on his face of a sad puppy. I felt sad for him, but knew I had to clear my thoughts before I committed to him.

That weekend at Grandma V's, I remembered a series of dreams I'd had several months earlier. For three consecutive nights I'd had the same dream about meeting this guy. I did not know him, I had not met him prior to this, but in the dreams I knew his name. It was Charlie.

That's when I realized the dreams had been a prophecy, God's way of saying it was going to be okay. He is "the one." After all, he and his family truly loved me. They cared about my well-being and they cared about each other. They were the kind of family I wished I had grown up with, and now, after so much pain and struggle, I would finally be getting my heart's desire.

Upon returning, I simply said, "Yes, I will marry you."

His eyes shining, Charlie wrapped his arms around me and held me tight, and for the first time ever, I felt like I was truly home.

My Forever Family

That summer, just seven months after we met, Charlie and I were married. Our daughter Naomi arrived that winter, followed by our other daughter Elizabeth, twenty-two months later. Seemingly overnight, I had gone from an abandoned youth to a grown woman with a husband who truly loved me for who I was and two little miracles with whom God had chosen to bless us. Before giving birth to them I never could have imagined feeling such a deep love for another person. Each day, my heart overflowed with gratitude that He had entrusted us with these amazing beings. It was a privilege and honor I have never taken lightly.

Having children also brought a new understanding of the covenant, "Till death do us part." These words were not just about building my relationship with Charlie, but with our entire family, including the one he had grown up with. In time, I grew closer with his brothers, all of whom readily accepted me as one of their own and never, ever judged me. Calvin and Ruth were like parents to me, always there with arms wide open, loving me unconditionally. "Momma Ruth" was always there to lend an ear when one needed it. She genuinely cared for people and never once asked for anything in return.

My new family introduced me to many things, most of which were fun, pure, and simple. I may have been a young adult but in truth I was still that child who yearned to experience joyful abandon and to be accepted. One of my favorite activities was our water battles. As most of these battles go, they started out small, usually with a spritz of water, then escalated to include a garden hose and an indoor kitchen sink sprayer, with one person hiding behind the corner with the hose and another inside the kitchen door, ready for whatever awaited them. There was always plenty of water on the kitchen floor, drenched bodies, and side-splitting laughter. As for the actual children, they would be splashing around in their kiddie pool while their "Pop Pop" sat a few feet away in his lawn chair, singing his whimsical songs to them.

Occasionally, I ask myself why God would see fit to bless me with such a beautiful family. Then I am reminded that He wants to give all His children the desires of their hearts. I feel overwhelmed at times in the realization of what an amazing family He has granted me the privilege to be a part of.

Other than that short trip to New York with Mike and Pap, I had never had vacations as a child; now they were a fairly regular occurrence that included extended family. We'd head to the beach, joined by aunts, uncles, cousins, and grandparents all in the same place. Everyone would work together to dig a huge hole in the sand until we saw water pooling in the bottom, but nothing topped my daughters' squeals of delight when they buried "Daddy Charlie" in that hole and placing chips around him for the seagulls to come eat.

We can't forget Great Grand-mom, better known to the family as "GG-mom," floating on her inner-tube out in the ocean without a care in the world while the aunts and uncles were out fishing for flounder for the evening meal. Even amidst all this excitement there were many times when I stopped and just took it all in, my heart overflowing with joy. For the first time I was witnessing the togetherness a real family could have and should have, and I'd have to remind myself I was not just a witness—*I was a part of it.*

See what great love the Father has lavished on us, that we should be called children of God! And that is what we are!
~ 1 John 3:1a NIV

"So I say to you, ask and it will be given to you; seek, and you will find; knock, and it will be opened to you. For everyone who asks, receives; and he who seeks, finds; and to him who knocks, it will be opened. …how much more will your heavenly Father give the Holy Spirit to those who ask Him?" ~ Luke 11:9,10,13 NAS

My new life went much deeper than just fun and games. In time, I came to understand that Charlie was never going to leave me. No matter what I was going through, no matter how hard things got, he chose to stay by my side. He chose to love me in my darkest times. His love has proven to be steadfast and I would remain awestruck that God had seen fit to gift me with this amazing man.

My husband had heard about most of the abuse I had experienced as a child. Even though he listened to my stories I don't think he understood the impact it would have on our future relationship and what role it would play in our lives together. Truth be told, neither did I.

When the girls were two and four my perfect life began to unravel. Momma Ruth and Grandma V were both diagnosed with the dreaded "C", and within a matter of months I lost two pillars in my life. Suddenly, nothing seemed to make sense, and I felt adrift for the first time since marrying Charlie. It was through the devastation of loss and the process of dealing with their deaths that God allowed healing to begin in my life.

When they passed away, God began to take me on this amazing journey back so that I may truly move forward in my life. It was then that God reminded me I did not need to constantly look back. It was then that I realized how much pain I had suffered, and how important it was that I did not pass the pain along to my children. I also realized I wanted to help other children so that I might save them from having to live the type of life I lived.

With God's support I was also able to help Calvin—or Dad, as I had come to call him. Joseph and Elmer had gone off to college and without Ruth around, Dad had let the house, and his health, deteriorate.

Charlie, the girls, and I moved in with him, thinking we would bring whatever joy we could to the time he had left. I spent a good three months cleaning things out, painting, and redecorating to make it look like a nice home again. Though he missed Ruth terribly, the girls brought life into the place and a smile to his face. Whatever we gave to him, we received tenfold, and I remain very grateful to have spent that last year with this kind, gentle soul.

Most of all, I felt blessed to have had such wonderful parents, even if only for a short time.

33 Children

It was a difficult Christmas. Dad had passed away days before but we still needed to make it a fun day for the girls. The entire family gathered together, each of us doing our very best. After the holidays were over and our everyday routine resumed, it seemed even harder to move on. Ruth and Calvin had left a gaping, undeniable hole in our lives.

Then one day my husband came to me and said, "I know the perfect job for you."

"I didn't know I was looking for a job," I replied with a smile.

"I think you'll like this one."

"Okay," I conceded, "What is it?"

"I think we should do foster care."

I drew back in surprise. By this time Charlie and I had been married ten years, and for most of them I'd been asking him to foster children. He'd always said no.

"You better not be kidding around, because you know I will do it right away."

He promised me he was serious. In fact he'd been thinking about it for some time, and suddenly the time seemed right.

Now we had another decision to make: to stay in Dad's house or buy a new home for ourselves. After much discussion we devised a plan. We would look for two totally different types of homes—a small one for just the four of us and a large one with lots of bedrooms that we could fill up with children—and trust that God would lead us to the right one.

Sure enough, we found a small Cape Cod house with three bedrooms, and a large double house with six bedrooms.

Once we saw the steps in the double house we knew we had found the right home. For me, it was a dream come true, literally.

There have been several times in my life when God spoke to me through my dreams, the most important of which was when I dreamt of Charlie before we met. I don't know why He chooses this means of communication, but I have always been grateful for it. It's like He's giving me a "heads-up" about some opportunity or choice I will have to make. About six months before Charlie and I decided to look for a new home, I had had a dream. In the dream there was a home with two sets of steps which were, oddly, side by side. One set of steps was rather nondescript; the other, however, was definitely eye-catching, with red carpeting that had a unique design. When I woke up the next morning my immediate thought was, who in the world would have a house with two sets of steps side by side, and who would put that ugly carpet on them? Whoever they were, their taste in décor left a lot to be desired. I then dismissed the dream and gave no further thought to it until the day our realtor led us to the six-bedroom house.

During the course of our tour that day we had gone upstairs to look at the bedrooms. As we went to head back down the steps I noticed that they didn't look the same. I asked the realtor about it and he said, "Oh, there are two sets of steps side by side. We came up one side and are going down the other."

From my vantage point at the top of the steps I looked down the right side, then down the left, unable to believe what I was seeing. It was just like my dream! Though it would clearly take a lot of work to turn the double home into a single six-bedroom home, I knew without a doubt that this was where we were meant to be.

One month later we moved in. As expected the renovations were significant, however, with all the changes we made we never touched the two sets of steps, including the unique red carpeting. It would remain there until one month before we decided to sell the home some ten years later.

After settling in we began phase two of our plan: we opened our home to foster children. Over the next twenty years we were given the opportunity to love and care for thirty-three boys and girls.

It is difficult to put into words the incredible blessing being a foster parent has been. In every child's face I could see my own experiences, first being abused and abandoned by my mother, father, and stepmother, then being shuffled from foster family to foster family without ever really connecting to them. This, I vowed, would never happen to any of our foster children. When a child entered our home, he or she instantly became part of our family. No matter where we went or what we did they were included and loved as if they were born to us. In allowing me to care for them, I realized, God was helping me to heal the damage to my own inner child.

After several children had spent time in our home before being placed with their relatives, I began to pray that God would send a child to adopt. I asked for a little boy that my husband would bond with over sports and other father-son things. I asked that we would connect with him just as if he was our very own.

Three days later we received a call asking if we would consider taking in a toddler. His father had brought him to the agency asking them to find his son a good home because he wasn't able to care for him. There was no hesitation; I didn't even call Charlie to ask his opinion, as I usually did every time we were told of a child. I just said, YES! YES! YES!

It was love at first sight when he arrived. Just as I had prayed, John was a natural fit with everyone in our family. Just as I had prayed, the bond between him and Charlie was immediate and strong as steel. What amazed me the most, though, was that my prayer around their love of sports was answered.

Shortly after John's adoption was finalized he began asking for a brother. I again went into prayer, this time asking God to send us another boy, one who didn't come with too much baggage. As Charlie and I grew older some of the issues the children came with had become harder to deal with, so I asked for a child who needed love and care but had not experienced so much abuse.

Once again, God granted my request to a tee. The agency called to ask if we would consider a newborn baby, one who was available for adoption. In all our years fostering it was the only other time I said yes without calling Charlie. We were being given a newborn, a child with no baggage, to raise as our own. It was the answer to our prayers.

His name was Elijah, and while he had not suffered abuse it soon became apparent that he did have some special needs. After fostering thirty children, one becomes adept at recognizing when something isn't quite right. It wasn't so apparent to the system, and it would take nearly five years before we got an official diagnosis.

I will never forget how on the day of Elijah's adoption his case worker pulled me aside and asked, "Are you sure you want to go through with this?"

I asked her why she would ask me that. Considering all I had been through I don't know why I was surprised by the question.

"Most people would not have kept him," she replied, "He would have become one of the statistics that get bounced around from home to home."

"Then it's a good thing God placed him in our home," I said, "and yes we are sure we want to go through with the adoption."

Clearly, things had not changed from when I was growing up. Children who are less than "perfect" are deemed disposable, and they will continue to be until someone stands up for them. That is not to say it's always been easy. Over the years we've faced our share of challenges—and then some—but I would not change our journey for anything. Learning about and dealing with special needs/disabilities has been a huge learning experience for our entire family. I often pray for God to bless Elijah with the abilities to become the man He has created him to be. I know that one day our son will become that man, and in the meantime I watch him grow with joy in my heart.

This year, after two decades of fostering, Charlie and I agreed it was time to retire. It was a bittersweet decision. Caring for children has been a huge part of who I am, and despite the considerable trials, an amazing gift. I sometimes wonder whether God did so in spite of my past or because of it, but whatever His reasoning I am eternally grateful for it. Each of those children holds a special spot in my heart, just like we hold a special spot in God's heart. I could tell you all the stories of their lives and what they've been through and how their lives have impacted my own. Many tears have been shed for these children, and many prayers have been offered on their behalf. Maybe one day we will meet again—oh, what a blessing that would be! Until that day, I remain open to whatever blessings lie ahead.

> *Come, you who are blessed by my Father, take your inheritance, the kingdom prepared for you since the creation of the world. For I was hungry and you gave Me something to eat, I was thirsty and you gave Me something to drink, I was a stranger and you invited Me in, I needed clothes and you clothed me, I was sick and you looked after Me. ... "Truly I tell you, whatever you did for one of the least of these brothers and sisters of mine, you did for Me."*
>
> *~ Matthew 25:34-36 & 40 NIV*

The Journey Forward

Over the past twenty-plus years God has continued to amaze me in all that He does and provides, not only for me but my entire family. Despite all the painful, and some would consider insurmountable, things that have happened to me, God has chosen to restore and bless.

Of all the questions I have asked God over the years, the one that remains forefront in my mind is why He would choose to bring me such profound healing. Not only has He brought me to a place of knowing I am forgiven, He has used me to do His work in a myriad of ways, including being responsible for the funds for Women's Ministry and Youth Ministry. Most recently, I was made treasurer for an entire district of twelve churches. I did not seek any of these positions out, rather, they were offered to me by the church leaders. As a youth I often asked *Why me?* when some painful circumstance befell me. These days, I ask the same question, but it is with gratitude and wonder that He has chosen me for such blessings. I don't demand an answer; I simply rest assured that it has all been part of His plan. He is all about restoration, and I have most certainly been restored.

For there is nothing hidden that will not be disclosed, and nothing concealed that will not be known or brought out into the open. ~ Luke 8:17 NIV

I no longer want to live a life in bondage to those who hurt me. I no longer want to feel imprisoned by the guilt and shame. I definitely no longer want to feel hatred towards others.

What I've come to realize is that when you hold hatred or anger in your heart toward another person, you are held captive, like a prisoner. But when you release that person from your hatred and anger, then you are free and no longer held captive.

As Max Lucado wrote so poignantly in his book, *And the Angels Were Silent*, "As long as you hate your enemy, a jail door is closed and a prisoner is taken. But when you try to understand and release your foe from your hatred, then the prisoner is released and that prisoner is you."

Although I cannot say my relationship with my father has been restored, I can say I have come to a place where I do have unconditional love for him. I choose to live a life that is safe but my heart says he is worth loving. In loving my father, I find myself praying for him that he may someday be restored and experience the same deep loving relationship with Heavenly Father that I do.

Without a doubt, the person it was most difficult to release from bondage was Molly. During my healing journey I took part in Thom Gardner's Healing the Wounded Heart sessions. It was amazing what God brought to mind during those sessions. During the first one, we were asked to close our eyes and imagine we were in a room. We were then told to picture one piece of furniture. After a few minutes we were told to open our eyes and describe what we saw. Most everyone there announced that they saw a table.

Thom then explained the significance of "the table." It represents a place of rest, a place of peace. Jesus came to the table to fellowship with His disciples. We come to the table for connection with God. People long for the relationship God has designed for them in Christ; it's a place to rest in God to be present with Him and be filled with the love He has for us. The table is a place to build relationships with others. I raised my hand and asked him, "What if we can't see a table?" Being that I never experienced a place of comfort or rest or building of healthy relationships, it was not surprising. Well, my world changed that day. He asked me if I would be willing to do a healing session right there. My daughter Elizabeth was with me and he asked us to come to the front. As we sat there, with my eyes closed, holding my daughter's hand and seeing images in my mind, he asked what I saw and as I shared with him the visuals of my mind he assured me I was in a safe place and that Jesus was with me. One thing I remember about the experience was the grey fog my mom seemed to be wandering around in. For whatever reason she couldn't seem to find her way out. I wanted to save her but couldn't. It was about her making the choice to leave the fog she lives in. What came from the experience was that I had never forgiven my mother for leaving us and then again as a teen for not fighting to keep me. But during the process I came to realize how much God loves her and that He has a crown for her in Heaven. All she has to do is accept it. It's her choice. I also came to realize there's a crown in Heaven for me and I could envision what it looked like. Once the exercise was over he asked me to close my eyes again and to imagine the same room I had been in before, then asked if I could see a table now. At that moment I saw the most beautiful table I had ever seen in my life. It went as far as the eye could see and was filled with dishes for endless people to sit at the table and enjoy time together.

Several years later I was at a small shop and on the wall was a picture that looked very similar to the vision I had that day with Thom. I purchased the picture and it now hangs on my kitchen wall as a daily reminder that it is good to take time to rest and share life and God's love with others. I also went to visit my mom shortly after this session. We shared a walk around a local park and talked. I shared with her what happened and what God showed me in that vision. As I shared the fact that God had a crown for her and all she had to do was accept it, she broke down and began crying. It was the first time I'd ever seen her cry. Someday I pray she will accept the gift waiting for her.

At later sessions I took part in several other healing sessions with Pastor Matthews, a man so humble we often teased him about it.

After my second healing session he asked me if I felt I was on the right path. I told him that yes, I know I am, but there was still one person I needed to find healing from. That one person was Molly.

"I know I need healing," I said, "but she doesn't deserve forgiveness and I am not ready to forgive her."

That was going to be a big step, and I didn't know when, if ever, I would be ready.

My prayer is that someday, I will have the chance to meet ALL of my family in Heaven. What a glorious day that will be. I believe my Heavenly Father, my Daddy God, knows the desires of my heart and somehow He WILL allow this to happen. I know it's the desire of His heart too.

Until that day, I choose to do my best in being the person God has created me to be. The person who loves others and themselves.

Love the Lord your God with all your heart and with all your soul and with all your mind and with all your strength. …love your neighbor as yourself. ~ Mark 12:30-31 NIV

How Big is Your God

Seven years ago, I found myself at a Women's Retreat. I was not there for myself, but rather for my friend Dawn. Going to these retreats was her favorite thing to do and as she did not have transportation I promised I would get her there. After others heard about it, they asked to go too. During the retreat they all received what God had intended for them. On the last day I sat there feeling like it was a nice retreat, but that I really didn't feel like God had spoken to me in any special way. I began to wonder what I was even doing there.

Still I figured there had to be a purpose, so I began to pray that He would show me what He had intended me to receive. It was then that the guest speaker Luann began talking about world missions. She invited people to join her on any of her upcoming trips.

As I listened, still nothing said *this is it*, because in reality I never intended to leave the United States. While I enjoy traveling to other states, other countries didn't interest me.

Then it happened. She began to talk about a trip to Greece. It was like I couldn't even stay in my seat. I wanted to jump up and shout, "I will go!" My mind began to race thinking about all the things that needed to be done in order to go. I didn't even have a passport. And the price was so high! My husband would never agree to spend that much money. On the other hand, it would be the perfect way for our son John, who was Greek, to experience the country, the culture, and its people.

After the retreat was over, I could no longer contain myself.

I ran up to Luann and asked her if I went on the trip whether I would be able to take my son. I was a little surprised when she told me that I could. I then asked her for the details and explained I couldn't commit right there because I'd have to talk it over with my husband. I told her I honestly didn't think he would say yes, and that he'd probably say, "Only if you can raise all the money, because we don't have it."

Upon arriving home, I immediately told Charlie about the mission trip to Greece. He listened intently. When I told him the cost would be $4,000 if John and I both went, his response was as expected, "We can't afford that."

"What if God provided us the money for the trip?"

"If God provides every penny," he replied, "you can go."

As confident as I've ever been, I told our son we would be going to Greece. We started sending letters asking for any support—including prayer—people could give us. The response was overwhelming. Some people sent money, while those who could not afford to sent stuff for us to sell on eBay; still other sent prayers.

What amazed me the most about the eBay sales was that everything people donated sold for the largest amounts. The items we found at yard sales sold, but for less money than those given with love.

One day I received an email that simply stated: "I have sixty-six thousand flyer miles. If you can use them, they are yours." This was enough to purchase a direct flight to Greece. You ask, how does that happen? I say only God speaking to the hearts of others can make that happen.

Through it all, God not only provided every penny, but the passports were paid for as birthday gifts. Then I found out I had never received shots as a child. Although you don't need more than the basics to go to Greece I still needed to get a few shots. I found out I could get them all free at a local clinic if I allowed them to test for HIV. My HIV test came back negative and I received all the shots I needed. Yes, God is good.

God even enlisted my sister Emily. When she first heard about the cost she was skeptical, so I was surprised when one day she handed me an envelope. She told me that God had convicted her and this was the amount He had told her to give. She wasn't the only one who seemed to have been directed by God to give rather large donations.

This is how God blesses His children, when they are obedient to His calling/nudging.

Just two weeks before we were to leave, I received an email from Luann. There were updates on the trip, including the fact that we would be ministering to several groups of gypsies.

As I read it, my heart sank and I began to panic. I'm not sure why, but I had this preconceived notion about gypsies and how they were not very nice people.

It also said I should consider bringing some handcrafted items to give to the people we would be ministering to. I once again turned to our church family and asked for donations.

One day Dawn knocked on my door and handed me a large garbage bag. "This should help you on your trip."

I thanked her, filled with gratitude and very aware that in a way she was the reason I knew about this trip in the first place. It was only after she left that I opened the bag and stared down at the contents in dismay. It was a bag full of yarn. Oh no, I thought, she misunderstood. Now what am I going to do with this?

Then, without thinking, I dumped out the bag of yarn and

noticed the partially begun afghan at the bottom. I sighed. Molly had taught me how to crochet, but I didn't want anything to do with anything she taught me. I said, "Okay, God, if I can figure out this pattern I will finish it."

Well, not only did I figure it out, I was able to make an entire suitcase full of items to give to those we would meet in Greece.

Talk about how big our God is! The entire time I crocheted that afghan, I prayed. I prayed for Molly, I prayed for the ladies we would be meeting and their families, I prayed for forgiveness, I prayed for healing and I prayed for God's love to cover them all.

As I went on the trip my fears subsided, until I met up with Luann in Greece. At the airport she told me I should write out my testimony and that she would like me to share it at several of the meetings we would attend. What had I gotten myself into? How could I possibly share my testimony? The bigger question, how could I let the same God who provided for this trip down? He obviously wanted us here for a reason.

Despite my trepidations, I wrote it all down and handed it off to Luann. My relief was short-lived, however. When she saw what I wrote, she told me I needed to shorten it. I told her I had never done this before so I wasn't sure what I should take out. I gave her what I had written and asked her to shorten it for me. About an hour later, she came back and told me to keep it as it was and that I would be sharing it at every meeting we went to.

Talk about a roller coaster of emotions and fear! I just knew I had to do it. I was in a foreign country and no one knew me, so it didn't matter what they thought of me afterwards. Once again I did as I was asked.

We ended up doing several meetings in Greece, then

traveling on to Bulgaria. I shared my testimony at each one, and the response was overwhelming. At a place in Sophia, Bulgaria, after I had shared my story, it was time for open prayer. We would pray for anyone who requested it. I stood there stunned when most everyone in the room came up and asked me to pray with them. The pastor of the church asked them to spread out to the other two ladies who were there. I asked God to help me pray with these ladies and He did. In all the praying I felt like Moses standing on top of the mountain in the presence of God and I never wanted to come down. I wanted to stay there forever in His splendor and glory.

At the conclusion of another meeting in Gotse Delchev, Bulgaria, some of the women got up to thank us for coming. The one women said, "Thank you for sharing your story and your tears."

She then went on to say, "We cry all the time and it feels like no one ever hears us, but now we know that God does."

This was a group of the gypsies I'd been so afraid of. Not only were they outcasts in their society but as new believers in Christ they were also outcasts in their own communities.

My prayers over that crocheted blanket were heard by God. The gypsies needed to hear how much He loved them no matter what trials they'd been through. Through those prayers, I was also able to begin to forgive my stepmother for what she had done to me. Through those prayers I was able to be at peace in a foreign country sharing my story with others.

About a month after I returned I felt God's nudging to sit down and write. As I did I felt Him tell me to send it to a friend who happens to be a publisher. It was just a short article and I told her, "Do whatever you want with it, I'm only writing because I felt God tell me to do it."

About six months later she called to ask for my social security number. I asked her what she needed it for and she said they needed it so they could pay me. I was like WHAT! I told her, I wasn't looking for money. She said, "We are publishing it and we pay people who send in articles that we publish."

Once again feelings of being overwhelmed filled my heart.

The article was in fact published and a few months later I received another phone call. This time a gentleman was on the other end and he said, "My name is Harvey so and so and I am calling to find out when you are going to write your book."

"Yeah, right, who is this?" I figured it was a friend playing a joke on me.

"No, this is real, my name is Harvey so-and-so and I am calling to find out when you are writing your book."

I thanked him for calling but informed him I would not be writing a book.

He proceeded to suggest I write an outline and see what happens.

"I really am not writing a book, Harvey, but thank you."

He ended the conversation by asking if he could call me back in three months to see how the book was coming along.

I laughed, and said, "Sure, Harvey, you can call me back if that's what you'd like to do."

With that we said our goodbyes, and I forgot all about Harvey and the random phone call.

Three months later I woke up one morning with God nudging me to write again. Not knowing for certain what I was going to be writing about I went to my computer and began typing.

The words just started coming out of nowhere and before I knew it I had typed eighteen pages. When I was done typing

I sat back and looked at what I had written. The thought came to mind, now that looks like the beginning of a book. The next day the phone rings. I say hello and instantly I hear, "This is Harvey so-and-so calling to see how you are doing on the book."

In utter astonishment, I replied, "NO WAY! I can't believe you are calling."

"You told me I could call back and I told you I would call in three months to check on the book."

"I know, but I thought it was a joke."

"No, it is not a joke. How are you doing with the outline?"

Still quite stunned, I told him that just the day before I had sat down to write.

We chatted back and forth about the process and how to do different aspects of the writing. That was several years ago, and while I never heard from Harvey again, those eighteen pages would be the seed from which this book sprouted. First, though I had some unfinished business to deal with.

After spending all that time in prayer with the blanket I'd made for our trip to Greece, I knew it was time to find a way to forgive Molly. She still didn't deserve it—nothing had changed on that front—but I realized that for my own sanity I needed to let go of the chain of bondage I had been carrying around. I needed to release ownership of it. When I asked Pastor Matthews if he would help me again, he did not hesitate.

This particular Healing Prayer session was very different from the others I had experienced, and not only because it focused exclusively on Molly. It was also very *dark*. In sharing this I must emphasize that there is a clinical process to this and an individual should be properly trained and have a counseling background so as to not cause more trauma. Like the other sessions, this one began with me closing my eyes. I was then asked to share whatever came to my mind, but all I could see was blackness! I recalled the basement and how black it was. But I seemed trapped, so Pastor Matthews helped me find that safe place where Jesus was with me. As we proceeded through the journey, we came to a set of steps. And on those steps terrible things were happening to Molly. I recognized these steps to be those in the home she grew up in. They were the steps outside her parents' kitchen that led upstairs. I saw her as a young girl being hurt and realized she had then perpetuated the same abuse on me and my sisters. In allowing God to show me the truth, I came to a place of empathy for her and was able to release the anger I had stored up inside. Finally, I was free of the burden I had held onto all those years! I will never forget the horrible things Molly did, but I can say through lots of prayer that I have forgiven her and can move on with my life.

Writing this book, I realized, was another step in my healing, and in my mission to help others along the way. I know this is a choice, and my prayer is that if you are reading this book and have dealt with abuse of any kind, or if you've been hurt along your life's journey, you too will make that choice to forgive and surrender the healing process to God. Allow Him to lead you through the journey He has for you. Allow Him to bless you in mighty ways, in BIG God ways.

So many times we devalue who we are now by living in the shame of who we once were.

Therefore if anyone is in Christ, he is a new creation; old things have passed away; behold, all things have become new. Now all things are of God, who has reconciled us to

Himself through Jesus Christ, and has given us the ministry of reconciliation, that is, that God was in Christ reconciling the world to Himself, not imputing their trespasses to them, and has committed to us the word of reconciliation. Now then, we are ambassadors for Christ, as though God were pleading through us: we implore you on Christ's behalf, be reconciled to God. For He made Him who knew no sin to be sin for us, that we might become the righteousness of God in Him. ~ *II Corinthians 5:17-21 NKJ*

I pray you become the ambassador God created you to be. I pray you will find healing and step into the journey forward that God has for you. I pray you will find your story filled with blessings of peace and joy meant just for you.

Epilogue

While writing this book I was very aware that as much as I was revealing about my life, there were gaps in my recollection, either because I was too young to understand what was happening or because decisions and events occurred without my consent or knowledge. I had accepted this fact; however, as the story continued to unfold, and more memories surfaced, I would often be hit by a flood of emotions just as raw as the day I took the road trip with my mother and Josephine. Those who had been a part of that history also stepped forward to share their perceptions, which brought even more pieces together. I never expected my book to open this proverbial can of worms, but I feel blessed that it has brought more darkness to light, and ultimately, is facilitating more healing.

When possible, I also reached out to those from my past who could help fill in the blanks. Some of this information from foster parents has been included where appropriate throughout the book. There were some questions, however, I felt could only be answered by the aunt I'd lived with for a time. I sent her an email with those questions and we set a time to talk.

We began the conversation with the usual, *Hi, how are yous?* then got right into the purpose of the call. She had already written out her answers and thought it was easier just to read them to me. First, she confirmed much of what I had recalled from early childhood. My mother left us when I was two years old, and though she moved about for several years she did stay in the general area. During that time she gave birth to Andy, the brother who was eventually adopted by my aunt and uncle.

My aunt also confirmed that Mom moved to Cincinnati when she was pregnant with Emily, apparently so no one could take the baby away from her. This would have been approximately two years before we moved to the farm and one year before Josephine and I received the bikes for Christmas. I was around six years old, which meant that for four years my mother had been in close proximity to us but not active enough in our lives for me to recognize her.

My aunt then moved on to the time when I lived with her and my uncle, specifically sharing about how terrible I was.

When she had finished reading, she asked, "Did I upset you?"

"No, I'm not upset." It was an honest answer. Although my aunt's words were difficult to hear, they were true. I had always known I needed help back then, but until that moment I hadn't realized how desperately.

"Sarah needed professional help," she recited as if reading my mind, "Sarah was belligerent and defiant. Sarah stole money from our daughter and ate all the food that had been set aside for my husband when he returned home from work."

When she was finished I apologized for what I had done all those years ago. The conversation was also enlightening for her. It seemed neither she nor anyone else outside our parents' homes knew the extent of the depravity going on behind closed doors. Moreover, they didn't hear about it, even after my aunt and uncle adopted Andy, even after my sisters and I were placed in foster care.

As the call was winding down, I asked her what she and my uncle were told the day they were asked to take me in.

When she said, "Nothing," I was surprised; I had always assumed the cops had at least given them some information. Instead, my aunt assumed that all three of us older girls had been removed from Mom's house. I corrected her on that and told her about the beating I had sustained from Phyllis. I also told her how the police had taken me to the hospital, then to the police station the next day.

As we said our goodbyes, I realized I was no longer upset that my aunt and uncle eventually called CPS to have me removed from their home. They felt they needed to protect their own children. They had no way of knowing their actions would lead to my being placed in seven foster homes and two institutions over the next three years. Though there were a few exceptions along the way, all anyone seemed to see when they looked at me was a child out of control, a runaway, and a thief.

The truth is, like so many foster children, I was in desperate need of love and direction. I needed stability, something that would take a long time for me to find.

***

Sixteen years after the first trip to visit our childhood homes, I once again called on my mother to direct me to the rundown farmhouse in the middle of nowhere. This time was different. As we sat in my car staring out at the house I asked my mother if she could tell me why she left.

She hesitated, then suggested I might talk to someone else who knew what had happened and could give me the details I was looking for. I explained to her that I really preferred to hear it from her, since it's her story.

Finally, a breakthrough: she agreed to share the story. She

slowly began telling me how she would go to work every day while my father stayed home to console his cousin Renee, who was recently divorced and living with us at the time. Mom went on to say that Renee and my father were having an intimate relationship.

So, I thought, Molly had actually been telling the truth about that.

That winter, a major snowstorm hit, stranding my mother at my father's sister's house. After three days, she was finally able to make it home, exhausted and badly in need of rest. When my father told her to make a grocery list, she suggested Renee make the list since she knew what they needed.

My mom was on the edge at that point because she knew what my father was doing right in their own home but felt helpless to stop it. When he and Renee went to the grocery store she finally broke down. She couldn't take it anymore. It was her birthday and she told me she wrote my dad a note that said, "I'm tired of this and I'm not spending my birthday in this h- - - hole." Although there was still a foot of snow on the dirt road that led to the house, she managed to once again trudge through it until she was able to reach the main road where she called a friend for a ride into town.

My mom then commented that Molly had years to turn us girls against her. It was then that I realized she had no idea what the truth was.

"Mom," I said, "there were no conversations about you. Molly and Dad never talked about you or turned us against you. In fact Molly was the only mother I knew until the visit to Grandma's house that summer you came back." I told her she could read about it in Chapter 10.

When I asked her where she'd been all that time, she said she had moved from place to place for several years. In fact she made a list for me that contained thirteen addresses. She finally settled in Cincinnati until a year after Josephine went to live with her.

My mom seemed to think this story is filled with lies about her that Molly told us. I assured her that is not the case. I told her the only thing I remember is Molly parking down the street from the one house she lived in and stalking her. My job was to watch out the back window of the car to see if there was anything going on in the upstairs apartment. I didn't realize, though, who we were spying on.

A look of relief flashed across her face, then she asked, "So this is a story basically about your experiences?"

I nodded. "Yes."

She sat back in her seat, looking more comfortable than she had been since we'd begun the trip.

After discussing other aspects of my childhood, the topic turned to Josephine and how she had ended up going to live with Mom. My mother said she was contacted by Molly and told they were having problems with Josephine and asked if she would take her. Years ago, my dad's sister told me she had heard Josephine ran away. I was told before going to school the day she left, that she was sick. Oh, the tangled web we weave. Sick, running away, having problems all because you didn't want to care for a child. Molly makes me feel like VOMIT!

I then asked my mom if there was anything she could share in her own words for the book. She replied, "You and Heidi were both dropped off at my house with bags of clothes that didn't even fit. I was left with three girls, all going through puberty at the same time and I wasn't equipped to handle it.

I never had great parenting skills, but I did my best to raise you girls."

In writing my story I've come to realize, it's not just about the outward appearance. We need to get to know each person on a deeper level. In getting to know my mom over the years, I've learned that she too has a past and no one knows her entire story except her. They may know bits and pieces or just the parts they want to know. Although I've tried to learn the whole story, she has not been able to open up freely about her experiences. Maybe she will eventually come to a place where she's ready to let it all go and be healed.

As I've recently written in my blog, "TWIGS," I pray she will come to know the beauty that lies within her and is just waiting to bloom.

I pray too that when that day comes I will be a witness to it.

While I know she still has a difficult time giving and receiving love, I hope she knows deep down she is lovable and loved.

***

If you recall in the dedication I stated, "To Josephine and Heidi, that they may find healing in the truth." In this too, God has answered my prayers, for at various points in this writing I reached out to both of my sisters in hopes of them being able to share their experiences and, hopefully, speed their own healing. There were also times when they contacted me.

A short time ago, Josephine asked me to meet her for dinner so we could speak privately. I immediately sensed a heavy conversation coming on, but I had no idea that God was about to use my book to help my sister in her own healing journey.

Josephine had recently been carjacked, and in the wake

of this traumatic experience she began having flashbacks of events from her childhood that she couldn't seem to make sense of. She knew I was writing the book and asked me to share it with her in hopes that her counselor would read it and help her decipher the disturbing images. We sat there for several hours that night, talking and crying and talking some more. The conversation moved from topic to topic, each more upsetting than the one before it, but there were two particular instances that caused my jaw to drop in disbelief.

"I remember we had to stand inside the basement door with the lights out until they decided we could come back out," she recalled, "At first we begged and pleaded for them to let us out, but after a while we realized that once our eyes adjusted it wasn't so scary. It helped too when we could see the light under the crack of the door."

I was astounded. She had repeated my recollection nearly word for word! For the first time I felt validated— this was not something I had made up on my own. It really did happen!

The other event that stood out in her memory was the electric fence. She remembered being afraid when we had to trim the grass around the fence, "Because we never knew if Dad was going to turn it on while we were trimming." The realization that I wasn't the only one who had those same feelings also left me speechless. It was also a deeply healing moment for both of us.

I have discussed the contents of this book more with Josephine than Heidi or Emily, probably because we experienced more of the same things together. And while my heart breaks to see my sister suffer, I know that...*Weeping may last through the night, but joy comes in the morning.* ~ *Psalm 30:5 NLT*

Josephine has also channeled her own pain into service for others. For most of her adult life she has cared for children at an Army base while their parents are going through training or serving our country. Her work is a testament to her loving spirit and her determination to overcome the past.

I love you, Twinny.

***

When I messaged Heidi, I was very surprised when she agreed to talk about our childhood. The fact that she was willing to open up to me brought a sense of, *finally*! Heidi has never spoken about our childhood, so this was a huge step forward for her. Throughout our lives I believed she'd somehow managed to escape the brunt of what happened to us as children. As she spoke, I realized with a heavy heart just how wrong I was.

First she told me how she remembered when she was little not being able to do some of the things Josephine and I did because she couldn't walk right and had to wear corrective shoes. As a toddler I also wore corrective shoes but apparently it affected her more than it had me. How awful it must have been for her, not being able to run and jump like most children.

Heidi also recalled being at our grandmother's house, the same one who burnt my hands, and playing outside in the grass where I used to find the tiny tile pieces I thought were treasure pieces. Heidi spent most of that time eating berries.

Heidi reminded me that once we moved into Molly's house, all we did was run around outside with no supervision— something I had completely forgotten about. We would run up and down the street in front of our house, playing and chasing each other. Molly often slept in, and each morning we would take whatever cereal we could find and eat it outside, or we would knock on neighbors' doors and ask for food. There was one neighbor in particular we frequently asked. She had two kids so maybe we figured she would have enough food for us. This memory lends credence to the statement I made to the teacher all those years ago. We really didn't have much food at home, or at least there was no one around to give it to us.

Heidi also recalled the electric fence punishments at the farm, and the beatings. She reminded me of the time, when she was about eight or nine, that she had her hands smashed in the big old black upright piano that sat on our enclosed front porch. Heidi was tinkering around on the piano when Molly came out and ordered her to place her hands on the keyboard; she then took the lid and smashed it down on my sister's hands. I had no idea what made Molly so mad; then again we rarely knew why she did anything or what would set her off.

Heidi even remembered the time my father shot at me. I was in shock when she said, "He acted as if it was a joke." I hadn't remembered any of my sisters being there, so for her to speak about that incident was overwhelming to me. Most devastating, though, was the revelation that Molly had also sexually abused Heidi, when she was about nine or ten years old. She shared small details of what Molly had done to her. As she spoke those words, tears streamed down my face. All these years I thought she had been saved from enduring that aspect of our childhood.

Everything ran together a bit after I was placed in foster care, but I was able to construct a rough timeline. Apparently Child Protective Services started coming to my mother's on a regular basis. The house was always a mess, including dog feces all over the kitchen floor. It was another job that I was expected to take care of, and one I quickly tired of, especially since it wasn't my dog. According to Heidi, CPS had found there was no food in the house and no supervision. There were, however, drugs.

I knew the babysitter had done some sort of drugs but I don't think I realized what it was at the time. Then after I came back from foster care I found some prescription drugs and marijuana in my mother's room. That's how Josephine and Heidi ended up in foster care.

As I mentioned earlier, both would return home long before me. Then one day Molly showed up and convinced Heidi she'd be better off going with her, just as she had done with me earlier on. Heidi went with her, only to find herself living, not with Dad and Molly, but with a friend of hers. As mentioned earlier, this was all a rouse to avoid paying child support; in fact, our father said he'd rather go back to jail than give my mother one cent. To stop this from happening Molly did whatever she had to do, including making it look as though we'd left of our own doing. Heidi was actually in the process of being adopted by her friends' parents when, on the day before it was to become finalized, the father was killed in a head-on collision. Everything fell apart, and Heidi was once again left with no one to love her.

After this she was bounced from place to place, including the home of the same aunt and uncle I had lived with. Then an incident happened and she ran away to Virginia, where she stayed in the bus terminal until she was able to contact Mom's other brother. He came and got her, only to ship her off a month later to North Carolina, where Mom's sister lived. Once that aunt moved north Heidi found herself back where she began. She ran away again, this time to me, asking for help. That's when Grandma V arranged for Heidi to live with her sister. She would stay there until she met Brad, whom she married within the week. She finally found her way out. She was free. Today Heidi is the proud mother of four amazing children and is expecting her eighth grandchild. Like me, she was also a foster parent, mostly to pre-teens, for many years. I pray she too knows, she is LOVED! I love you—forever.

***

As I also stated in the dedication, *Last but certainly not least, Emily.*

As adults Emily and I have spent countless hours processing and learning from each other about our growing up years. We've shared many tears and lots of hugs, as well as a lot of information that brought clarity and validation.

For many years I'd believed no one knew the truth about what happened that fateful night before I was placed in foster care. So many times, I'd asked those I thought would know, only to hear, "No," or "It's hard to remember."

Recently our families got together again. As the men hung out around the campfire, Emily and I sat inside talking. Time passed quickly as we caught up with all that was happening in our lives, talking until the wee hours of the morning.

One of those conversations brought forth more validation. I was telling her about the editing process and how recently many of my experiences in the book had been validated during conversations with other family members. Yet, surprisingly, no one seemed to remember or know anything about the night I left our mother's home.

Emily gave me a puzzled look. "How could no one remember?"

"You mean you actually remember that night?"

"You mean the night Phyllis lost her sh--," Emily said, "The night she imploded?"

"Wow!" I said, "You *do* remember."

I told her how I had asked our mom, Josephine, and Heidi, and even our aunt, and no one seemed to know or remember anything.

Her response was one that I've been waiting to hear for a very long time.

"That old battle-axe was only looking out for her own interests and never cared about anyone of us except herself," she said.

I listened intently as she described the screaming and yelling that took place and how Phyllis was knocking me around on the steps. Then, all of a sudden, it was over and they left. She finished by saying, "When we returned, you weren't there, I had no idea where you went."

She paused for a moment. "I don't understand how Mom could say she doesn't remember that night."

"Why do you say that?"

"Because Phyllis was screaming and at one point said to Mom, "It's either her or me! I'm not putting up with this !&$?% anymore, so if she comes back, I will leave."

According to Emily, our mother had just sat there listening to all the trash spewing forth from Phyllis's mouth.

"I didn't understand it," Emily added, "she chose Phyllis and you never came back."

I was shocked. Finally, someone else had remembered what I had experienced firsthand. Most surprising was the fact that my "witness" had at that time been just seven years old.

Just as Emily helped me heal with her revelations, she has over the years helped and ministered to countless others. She drove a bus for a local school. No one wanted that specific run because they said the students were too hard to handle. Emily has a way about her that speaks love to students who others choose to ignore. She loved her students and got to know them on a personal level. When a student whose mother was terminally ill needed a home, Emily opened her doors to him and his sister. She got to know their mother and made a promise to continue loving her children after she passed away.

She has an amazing heart and loves freely.

I love you, SIS.

It was for freedom that Christ set us free; therefore keep standing firm and do not be subject again to a yoke of slavery.

...For you were called to freedom, brethren; only do not turn your freedom into an opportunity for the flesh, but through love serve one another. For the whole law is filled in one word, in the statement, "You should love your neighbor as yourself."

...the fruit of the Spirit is love, joy, peace, patience, kindness, goodness, faithfulness, gentleness, self-control; against such things there is no law. ~ Galatians 5:1, 13-14, 22 NAS

May the God of hope fill you with all joy and peace as you trust in Him, so that you may overflow with hope by the power of the Holy Spirit. ~ Romans 15:13 NIV

I feel honored to be there for support and a shoulder to cry on for my sisters. It amazes me that as I complete this book, they now begin their journey forward. It truly is ALL in God's timing.

I pray they are victorious in overcoming their fears. I pray they feel the love that is offered to them at *any time*.

I pray as they take time to focus on their healing, that they find freedom from all the trauma they've experienced and find peace and joy in the end.

I am grateful to be at a place in my life where, although the events in my life are being validated and it hurts to hear them again, I no longer claim ownership of the chains of bondage they have caused. Those chains have been broken and I am FREE! Free to live a life filled with blessings, peace, and joy. I am free to live the life God has created for me to live filled with love. HIS LOVE!

I pray, you too can experience that freedom and love.

Now you are no longer a slave but God's own child. And since you are His child, God has made you His heir.
~ Galatians 4:7

ALPHA OMEGA GUIDE

Beginning - End

I've learned through the healing process that there are some basic steps a person can take to find healing and forgiveness through any situation. While not always easy, if done for each situation with a sincere heart, healing is the gift awaiting you. I pray you too will discover the blessings, peace, and joy.

In the beginning:

A – Admit. Accept the trauma/abuse happened.
Put on the full armor of God, so that you will be able to stand firm against the schemes of the devil. For our struggle is not against flesh and blood, but against the rulers, against the powers, against the world forces of this darkness, against the spiritual forces of wickedness in the heavenly places. ~ Ephesians 6:11-12 NIV

L – Lament. Grieve the loss.
Now is your time of grief, but I will see you again and you will rejoice, and no one will take away that joy. ~ John 16:22 NIV
Blessed are those who mourn, for they will be comforted. ~ Matthew 5:4 NIV

P – Pray. Ask for healing and the ability to forgive.
"For I will restore health to you and heal you of your wounds," says the Lord. ~ Jeremiah 30:17 NIV
"So do not fear, for I am with you; do not be dismayed, for I am your God. I will strengthen you and help you; I will uphold you with my righteous right hand." ~ Isaiah 41:10 NIV

H – Honor. Give praise to Jesus/God.
Now may the God who gives perseverance and encouragement grant you to be of the same mind with one another according to Christ Jesus, so that with one accord you may with one voice glorify the God and Father of our Lord Jesus Christ. ~ Romans 15:5 NIV

A – Appreciate. Give thanks, celebrate.
Give thanks to the Lord, for he is good; His love endures forever. Cry out, "Save us, God our Savior; gather us and deliver us from the nations, that we may give thanks to Your holy name, and glory in Your praise." Praise be to the Lord, the God of Israel, from everlasting to everlasting. ~ 1 Chronicles 16:34-36 NIV

In continuing to heal and grow:

O – **Omit. Continue to get rid of the negative.**
Whatever is true, whatever is honorable, whatever is right, whatever is pure, whatever is lovely, whatever is of good repute, if there is any excellence and if anything is worthy of praise, dwell on these things. The things you have learned and received and heard and seen in me, practice these things, and the God of peace will be with you. ~ Philippians 4:4-9 NAS

M – **Maintain. Nurture (or cultivate?) healthy relationships.**
Therefore, as God's chosen people, holy and dearly loved, clothe yourselves with compassion, kindness, humility, gentleness, and patience. Bear with each other and forgive one another if any of you has a grievance against someone. Forgive as the Lord forgave you. And over all these virtues put on love, which binds them all together in perfect unity. ~ Colossians 3:12-14 NIV

E – **Encourage. Strengthen one another.**
Be kind to one another, tender-hearted, forgiving each other, just as God in Christ also has forgiven you. ~ Ephesians 4:32 NIV

G – **Give back. Help others along the way.**
Love the Lord your God with all your heart and with all your soul and with all your mind and with all your strength. ..."love your neighbor as yourself." ~ Mark 12:30-31 NIV

A – *Accept. Receive God's unconditional love.*
See what great love the Father has lavished on us, that we should be called children of God! And that is what we are. ~ 1 John 3:1a NIV

Then He will be with you through your journey to the end.

RESOURCES

Youth Accepted = *

National Hotline for Sex Trafficking
Call 1-888-373-7888
Text 233733
Live Chat
humantraffickinghotline.org

Alabama
The Wellhouse, Inc *
1-800-991-0948
1-800-991-9937
the-wellhouse.org
info@the-wellhouse.org

Arkansas
Partners Against Trafficking Humans
(PATH)
501-993-1641
Victim services 501-301-4357
pathsaves.org
info@ pathsaves.org

New Hope Youth Ministries *
501-777-5955
newhopeyouth.org
info@newhopeyouth.org

Arizona
Phoenix Dream Center *
602-346-8700
602-346-8701
phxdreamcenter.org
California

Generate Hope *
generatehope.org

Journey Out
818-988-4970
journeyout.org
info@journeyout.org

Project Hope-LA Dream Center *
877-632-7234
dreamcenter.org/outreach
213-273-7000
213-273-7029
fostercare@dreamcenter.org
info@dreamcenter.org

San Francisco Safe House
415-643-7861
sfsafehouse.org
info@sfsafehouse.org

Saving Innocence *
323-379-4232
savinginnocence.org
info@savinginnocence.org

Slavery No More
818-741-3101
slaverynomore.org
info@slaverynomore.org

Traffic911 *
817-575-9923
Traffic911.com

Colorado
Free Our Girls *
freeourgirls.org
info@freeourgirls

Restore Innocence *
719-425-9405
restoreinnocence.org

Florida
More Too Life *
941-227-1012
moretoolife.org
exec_a@moretoolife.org

One More Child +1 *
863-687-8811
children@onemorechild.org
onemorechild.org

Place of Hope *
561-775-7195 Palm Beach
561-653-8274 West Palm
Beach
561-483-0962 Boca Raton
561-775-7195 Lake Park
561-691-8881 Palm Beach
Gardens
561-775-7195 Hobe Sound
561-775-7195Port Saint Lucy
placeofhope.com

Illinois
Grounds of Grace
314-472-5942
hisgrounds@groundsofgrace.com
groundsofgrace.com

Magdalene House Chicago
magdalenehousechicago.org
info@magdalenehousechicago.org

Naomi's House
312-327-8600
moodychurch.org/naomis-house

Indiana
Julian Center
317-920-9320
juliancenter.org/#

Kansas
Veronica's Voice
816-483-7101
913-214-1401
veronicasvoice.org
admin@veronicasvoice.org

Kentucky
Refuge For Women
859-254-0041
refugeforwomen.org

Maryland
**Arrow Child & Family
Ministries** *
arrow.org
888-626-6664 Baltimore
410-882-9133 Baltimore
410-734-9319 Bel Air
410-297-4100 Belcamp
877-426-7840 Salisbury
410-677-0743 Salisbury
443-798-6310 Towson

**Faith Alliance Against
Slavery & Trafficking FAAST**
443-424-3260
faastinternational.org

Safe House of Hope
443-690-5585
safehouseofhope.org

Massachusetts & New Jersey
Amirah
781-462-1758
amirahnewengland.org
info@amirahnewengland.org

My Life My Choice *
617-779-2179
fightingexploitation.org
MLMCinfo@jri.org

Teen Challenge-Run For Freedom
508-408-4378
855-404-4673
tcnewengland.org/16616-2/

Michigan
Hope Project *
231-747-8555
hopeprojectusa.org

Minnesota
The Link *
612-232-5428
thelinkmn.org

Missouri
Exodus Cry *
816-398-7490
exoduscry.com
info@exoduscry.com
intervention@exoduscry.com
restoration@exoduscry.com

New York
Coalition Against Trafficking in Women
212-643-9895
catwinternational.org
info@catwinternational.org

Safe Horizons
General
212-577-7700
Domestic Violence Victims
800-621-4673
Family Crime Victims
800-866-4357
Rape/Sexual Assault Victims
212-227-3000
safehorizons.org

Sanctuary for Families
212-349-6009
sanctuaryforfamiles.org

The Center For Youth *
585-473-2464
Youth in Crisis
585-271-7670
888-617-5437
centerforyouth.net
info@centerforyouth.net

The Door *
212-941-9090
door.org
info@door.org

North Carolina
Darkness to Light
919-807-0800
ncfamily.org/darkness-to-light-nc-ministries-serve-trafficking-victims

On Eagles Wings Ministries
877-647-1230
oneagleswingsministries.org
info@oneagleswings

Redeeming Joy *
704-904-8525
redeemingjoy.org
info@redeemingjoy@gmail.com

Ohio
Grace Haven *
614-302-9515
gracehaven.me
info@gracehaven.me

Oregon
Janus Youth *
503-233-6090
janusyouth.org
feedback@janusyouth.org

Pennsylvania
Covenant House
215-951-5411
covenanthouse.org
info@covenanthouse.org

Dawns Place
215-849-2396
ahomefordawn.org
info@ahomefordawn.org

North Star Initiative
717-568-2701
northstarinitiative.org

Oasis of Hope
570-673-4544
oasisofhopeusa.org

Tennessee
End Slavery Tennessee *
615-806-6899
endslaverytn.org

Texas
Arrow Child & Family Ministries *
877-922-7769
281-210-1500
arrow.org
806-335-9138 Amarillo
979-848-1100 Angleton
817-672-2300 Arlington
512-407-9501 Austin
409-835-1864 Beaumont
325-646-4141 Brownwood
877-922-7769 Houston/Spring
806-784-0447 Lubbock
903-581-5605 Tyler
254-752-2100 Waco/Bryan/College

Elijah Rising
832-628-3439
elijahrising.org
admin@elijahrising.org
prayer@elijahrising.org

Redeemed Ministries
832-447-4130
redeemedministries.com
info@redeemedministries.com

Utah
Fight the New Drug
385-313-8629
fightthenewdrug.org

Virginia
Youth For Tomorrow *
703-368-7995
youthfortomorrow.org/Girls-On-A-Journey-Program

Washington
Mirror Ministries
509-212-9995 Hotline
509-783-5730
mirror-ministries.org
info@mirro-ministries.org

Shared Hope International *
866-437-5433
sharedhope.org
savelives@sharedhope.org

Washington DC
Courtney's House
202-525-1426
For Survivor by Survivor
202-423-0480
Courtneyshouse.org

Polaris Project
202-745-1001
Text - 2337333 BeFree
polarisproject.org
info@polarisproject.org

Multiple States
Bethany Christian Services *
bethany.org
AL, AR, CA, CO, DC, DE, FL,
GA, IL, IN, IA, KY, MD, MA, MI,
MN, MS, MO, NE, NH, NJ, NC,
NY, OH, OR, PA, RI, SC, SD,
TN VA, VT, WA, WV, WI, WY

Covenant House *
800-388-3888
covenanthouse.org
info@covenanthouse.org
AK, CA, FL, GA, IL, LA, NJ,
NY, MI, MO, PA, TX,
Washington DC, Guatemala,
Honduras, Mexico, Nicaragua

THORN *
wearethorn.org
info@wearethorn.org

SUPPORT MINISTRIES

To get to know me is to get to know what I believe and support. Over the years I've worked with and sponsored several great ministries. They have not only helped me in my growth but many others as well. The following are a list of ministries that support some amazing causes/efforts. I personally recommend all these ministries and pray you will find a way to support or become involved in any or all of them.

MISSION: Samaritan's Purse is a nondenominational evangelical Christian organization providing spiritual and physical aid to hurting people around the world. Since 1970, Samaritan's Purse has helped meet needs of people who are victims of war, poverty, natural disasters, disease, and famine with the purpose of sharing God's love through His Son, Jesus Christ. The organization serves the Church worldwide to promote the Gospel of the Lord Jesus Christ.

samaritanspurse.org

VISION: A world where every child is loved, safe and developing their God-given potential.

MISSION: Partnering with the global Free Methodist Church, we advocate for the spiritual, physical, cognitive, and social development of children.

childcareministries.org

VISION: To accelerate Christian ministry in the disability community.

MISSION: To communicate the Gospel and equip Christ-honoring Churches worldwide to evangelize and disciple people affected by disabilities.

joniandfriends.org

VISION: Arrow will become the preferred Christian provider of child welfare and educational services connecting church and government to serve vulnerable children and families.

MISSION: Helping Kids & Strengthening Families

arrow.org

MISSION: Our mission is to support women who are survivors of domestic sex trafficking by providing physical, psychological, emotional, and spiritual care through a Christ-centered focus.

northstarinitiative.org

Adult & Teen Challenge

MISSION: Christ-centered, faith-based solutions for youth, adults, and families struggling with life-controlling problems, such as addiction.

Freedom from addiction for adults, teens, and families.

teenchallengeusa.com

CEF

CHILD EVANGELISM
FELLOWSHIP®

Since 1937   *Reaching children worldwide*™

VISION: Our ministry vision is to reach Every Child, Every Nation, Every Day.

MISSION: Our mission is to evangelize boys and girls with the Gospel of the Lord Jesus Christ and to establish (disciple) them in the local church for Christian living.

cefonline.com

ACKNOWLEDGEMENTS

While this book is my personal journey through life as I knew it and am now living, by no means could I have completed it on my own accord. Therefore, I would like to take a moment and share my heartfelt thoughts.

Recently, the most popular words that have come from my mouth are "to God be the glory." Honestly, without His nudging I would never have written my story. I pray He is glorified in whatever happens with this book. I also pray for those who read this story, that they will in some way find healing at whatever point they are in their journey. This story is for you, to assure you that you are not alone!

To my wonderful husband and beautiful children, thank you for your never-ending support and encouragement. The day Charlie and I met should go down in history as the day my life began. Without you by my side and forever supporting my many impromptu, yet genuinely heart felt, jump in feet first ideas, I can't imagine what life would be like. God knew I would need a gentle, honest, loving man like you to keep me grounded. I am honored to call you my husband and my best friend. (Maybe we can make that book number 2.)

Now, some thirty-plus years later, who would have imagined life with four amazing children who are following God's call on their lives. I am blessed to call each one of you, Naomi, Elizabeth, John, and Elijah a gift from God. As we've walked this journey together and you've all watched my healing process unfold, I am grateful through all the painful healing moments your love has never failed. Each one of you have brought joy to my heart in watching you grow and mature and walk your own life's journey. I am blessed to be your mother.

Although we've shared many painful moments throughout our lives, it is with tremendous respect I say thank you to my sisters Josephine, Heidi, and Emily for being willing to open not only my life but yours to the world. As my story unfolds your lives too will be impacted by what lies within the pages of this book. While you could have said no, you have all been so brave and supportive. For that I am forever beholden. I want to say thank you to each one of you for being willing to talk through the editing process and share your perspective on what happened. Each one of you have brought clarity to some aspect of the story and validation that solidifies it really did happen. I pray you all know you are loved.

While for some it may be difficult to understand I want to acknowledge my mom Rosie. You had choices to make in life, although not always the best choices, still, you chose to give life to every one of your children. That speaks volumes, knowing you too have a story. I am thankful for life itself and our recent trips together where you have finally begun to share what lies within your heart. I appreciate the information you shared that verifies different aspects of this story even though you didn't know you were validating what was already written. I pray you will one day find healing from your hurts.

I can't forget my aunt and brother, Andy. To my aunt thank you for your support in helping to clarify a few of the events and timeline. I wish life could have been different for all involved. No matter what, I am thankful you had a heart and home to open to Andy. Thank you for having an adoptive heart and being willing to open your home to myself and Heidi along the way.

To Andy, thank you for being willing to share your part in my life's story. Although I don't see myself in the same manner I appreciate you thinking of me as a hero. And, even though I don't feel like a hero, I know it comes from your heart and that makes me love you more. I do pray you will find the answers you need and know you too are loved. As adults, we tend to find out who our true friends are. Although I have a nice healthy group of people I call friends, the first person who always comes to mind is my friend Debbie. As always, I thank you for being the heart of Jesus the day you helped save my life. Without your intervention this book would not have been written. I thank you for your friendship and constant prayers. You are a true friend whom I know will one day hear the words, "Well done, thy good and faithful servant." Keep praying and loving those who are sometimes hard to love. I'm sorry it took so long for you to know the entire story. Thank you for being willing to read it and for your continued support in writing a review.

In keeping with true friends, I am honored that Superintendent David Harvey and Pastor Matthews were part of my journey. You both were there to see the journey unfold at such a crucial point in my life. You offered unconditional love and support for years on end. I remember the day I walked into our adult Sunday School class an announced that God truly loves me. The look on your face, Superintendent Harvey, was priceless. It said, "She finally knows, she is loved." Another moment etched in my mind is the day you commented, "I can't figure out who filled your love tank (meaning my heart)." I simply stated, "It had to be God." I think you'll agree as you read the entire story. Thank you for your willingness to do the work God has set before you and your willingness to write a review. "Well done, thy good and faithful servant."

Pastor Matthews, you are a solid rock and awesome mentor. Thank you for allowing me to walk by your side and to learn from you all that comes with saying yes to God when He calls you to do His work. You may not know, but when people ask me who Pastor Matthews is, my response is that if you ever want to know the truth about who God is and what it is to live a life walking in His will it is Pastor Matthews. Thank you for being a humble servant and an awesome example. Thank you for all you've done to help me in my healing journey and for your willingness to read the entire story and write a review. "Well done, thy good and faithful servant."

Along life's journey we acquire new friends which would be people like Dawn, Susan, and Dan. A big thank you to my dear friend Dawn for your ongoing words of encouragement and the notes of support and cheer. Even though that first bag of yarn brought a bit of panic, I will always be grateful for the healing that came from all the crocheting that was accomplished in order to minister to others. Thank you for your continued love and support.

Then, sometimes you meet a beautiful person like Susan. She could be described as a flower always in bloom with a kind word to say about everyone. Your heart is overflowing and bigger than I could ever have imagined. Your quiver carries more love than anyone I've ever met. Not only from your own children but also the children you have blessed with a home and unconditional love. It is with a grateful heart I say thank you for agreeing to read my story and write a review.

Sometimes we meet friends in faraway places or on the mission field, which is where I met Dan. While I've only known you for a short time, your gentle spirit was a breath of fresh air in the sweltering heat. I am honored to have been placed on your team while we worked to help others bring normalcy back to their lives. I am thankful to you for opening your heart to Elijah and taking him under your wing. I am also thankful that you were willing to say yes when asked if you'd write a review. I look forward to the day we will once again be able to serve others together through Samaritan's Purse. Thank you for your help in this process.

I also must salute ARROW Child & Family Ministries for coming along side me and believing in my story. I don't understand how God works out all the details months in advance, but I am glad that He led me to your website. I have searched endless hours and have not found another ministry that seems to fit so well with what is written in the pages of this book. I look forward to working with you to raise awareness for the victims of child abuse, the need for loving foster homes, and bringing awareness to the overwhelming issue of sex trafficking. Thank you for believing in me.

A big shout out to my sister in-law Sheila. Without you I would not have come to know about Powerful You! Publishing. Thank you for sharing your connections and ongoing support for writing my story. You are a special person with a big heart and I am honored to call you my sister.

This brings me to the editing of *A Journey Back to Restoration*. I want to thank Betty for proof reading and giving me pointers to improve the writing process before submitting it to a publishing company. Thank you for your honesty and encouragement.

Thank you to the beautiful Miss Amanda for your part in editing all the blogs and internet posts that occurred during the publication process. Without you I'm not sure how many people would read what was posted. Thank you for your knowledge and assistance, support, and encouragement. You have a great talent and I pray you will be noticed and blessings will pour out beyond what you can imagine.

To those behind the process at Powerful You! Publishing.

Three individuals working together as a team Sue, Kathy, and Dana. What an awesome team you are. Kathy, I appreciate your ability to help with the internet issues and keeping the monthly requirements on track. Although I've never mentioned it, organization is very important to me and I appreciate how well you all work together.

Sue, you are a great communicator. I appreciate all you've done with staying in touch via phone and email to keep things moving along smoothly. I appreciate the ongoing relationship that seems to move beyond just being a publisher. One of the things that stood out the most is your recognition of words. In writing my story, I hadn't realized how much I like words. After speaking with you I feel a kindred spirit and say thank you for all you do in helping individuals bring their stories to life. Thank you for all your support and encouragement along the way. Thank you for believing in my story and for believing that many hearts will be moved by reading my book.

And of course, Dana, I honestly can't imagine having anyone else doing the editing on this book. You asked questions up front and fulfilled beyond my expectation what I had hoped to attain. As I've shared with you before, I feel like I've given you a skeleton and you made those bones come to life. You've breathed life into my story that has brought even me to tears, and I've already lived it. It has been a pleasure working with you. I can't begin to imagine the thoughts going through your mind as day after day you read through and edited my story. My heart goes out to you for your endurance and dedication to helping make it as real to others as possible. Thank you for the tremendous work you've done in helping bring A Journey Back to Restoration to life.

In what you've done, it reminds me of the story in Ezekiel 37 where God breathed life into the dry bones. Through that story others came to know God really is a Sovereign God who loved them. I pray through this story others will come to know the awesome healing power of our Loving Heavenly Father, Daddy God.

Thank you to everyone who has been a part of this journey, may you all be blessed in an exceedingly abundant way.

1 The hand of the LORD was on me, and he brought me out by the Spirit of the LORD and set me in the middle of a valley; it was full of bones. ² He led me back and forth among them, and I saw a great many bones on the floor of the valley, bones that were very dry. ³ He asked me, "Son of man, can these bones live?"

I said, "Sovereign LORD, you alone know."

⁴ Then he said to me, "Prophesy to these bones and say to them, 'Dry bones, hear the word of the LORD! ⁵ This is what the Sovereign LORD says to these bones: I will make breath enter you, and you will come to life. ⁶ I will attach tendons to you and make flesh come upon you and cover you with skin; I will put breath in you, and you will come to life. Then you will know that I am the LORD.'" ⁷ So I prophesied as I was commanded. And as I was prophesying, there was a noise, a rattling sound, and the bones came together, bone to bone. ⁸ I looked, and tendons and flesh appeared on them and skin covered them, but there was no breath in them.

⁹ Then he said to me, "Prophesy to the breath; prophesy, son of man, and say to it, 'This is what the Sovereign LORD says: Come, breath, from the four winds and breathe into these slain, that they may live." ¹⁰ So I prophesied as he commanded me, and breath entered them; they came to life and stood up on their feet— a vast army. ~ Ezekiel 37:1-10 NIV

ABOUT
SARAH ISAAC-SAMUEL

In Sarah's heart-gripping journey she shares it all; from despair, abuse, and abandonment to peace, wholeness, and abiding faith. Through her triumphs she wants others to know it is worth the journey, to heal and forgive. Her aspirations are for those hurting and afflicted to experience the same gift of healing, forgiveness, peace, and joy that she has found.

Website:
AJourneyBackToRestoration.com

Email:
sarah@ajourneybacktorestoration.com
journeybacktorestoration@gmail.com

POWERFUL YOU! PUBLISHING
Sharing Wisdom ~ Shining Light

Are You Called to be an Author?

Do you have a message to share with the world? Is it your purpose and calling to inspire, encourage, and motivate others? Have people told you, *you should write a book?* If you've answered yes, then now is your time to get published.

Whether you choose to write your own book or contribute to an anthology, we will be your guiding light, professional consultant, and enthusiastic supporter. If you see yourself as an author partnering with a publishing company who has your best interest at heart and with the expertise to back it up, we're the publisher for you.

We provide personalized guidance through the writing, editing, and publishing process. We offer complete publishing packages and our service is designed for a personal and optimal author experience.

We are committed to helping individuals express their voices and shine their lights into the world. Are you ready to start your journey as an author? Do it with Powerful You! Publishing.

Powerful You! Publishing
powerfulyoupublishing.com